A Truthful Heart

A Truthful Heart

Buddhist Practices for Connecting with Others

Jeffrey Hopkins

with a foreword by

His Holiness the Dalai Lama

Snow Lion Publications
ITHACA, NEW YORK

Snow Lion Publications
P. O. Box 6483
Ithaca, NY 14851 USA
(607) 273-8519
www.snowlionpub.com

Printed in USA on acid-free recycled paper.
Designed and typeset by Gopa & Ted2, Inc.

ISBN-10: 1-55939-290-8
ISBN-13: 978-1-55939-290-7

Library of Congress Cataloging-in-Publication Data

Hopkins, Jeffrey.
  A truthful heart : Buddhist practices for connecting with others /
Jeffrey Hopkins ; with a foreword by His Holiness the Dalai Lama.
      p. cm.
  Includes bibliographical references.
  ISBN-13: 978-1-55939-290-7 (alk. paper)
  ISBN-10: 1-55939-290-8 (alk. paper)
  1. Religious life—Buddhism. 2. Buddhism—Doctrines.
I. Bstan-'dzin-rgya-mtsho, Dalai Lama XIV, 1935- II. Title.

BQ4302.H67 2008
294.3'5677—dc22   2007039982

Acknowledgments

I would like to express my gratitude to Steven Neal Weinberger and the late Leah Judith Zahler for transcribing and initially editing materials used in this book.

CONTENTS

FOREWORD BY HIS HOLINESS THE DALAI LAMA

C OMPASSION IS a major theme of all Buddhist traditions. The Buddha taught about it directly, and many subsequent commentators in India and all the lands to which Buddhism spread have praised it. The great Indian scholar and spiritual practitioner Chandrakirti famously stated, "It is only compassion that is like the seed, the moisture that nourishes it, and the ripened fruit that can be enjoyed. Because of this I pay my respects first to compassion."

Buddhist literature is replete with works extolling the virtues of compassion and the ways and means to awaken and enhance it within ourselves. However, there are also many stories that show that no matter how much you have read or thought about it, it is the spark of experience that brings compassion to life. Perhaps this is because you can read and think in isolation, but life's experience takes place in the company of others.

Jeffrey Hopkins is an old personal friend who has been of

great help to me as an interpreter. As a scholar he has made a major contribution to deepening understanding of Tibetan Buddhism through his university teaching and his many publications. He has also, in the course of his work, had access to some of the greatest contemporary Tibetan teachers. But most important of all, he has, over the years, steadily tried to put what he has learned into practice. This book, *A Truthful Heart*, contains a personal account that Jeffrey has drawn from classes and seminars he has given over the last thirty years or so. What I believe readers will find especially valuable is that the book contains the flavor of experience. It shares those glimpses and sparks of understanding that may inspire others to try the practices out for themselves.

I believe that compassion, a sense of kindness and warm-heartedness toward others, is the basic source of all happiness. Therefore, I have no doubt that every individual who attempts to cultivate it contributes to creating a happier, more peaceful world.

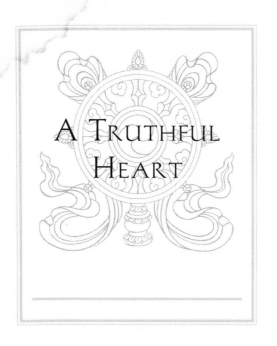

A Truthful Heart

INTRODUCTION

I GREW UP in Barrington, Rhode Island, and my most intriguing memory is of literally jumping off my moving bicycle into a ditch to aid a fallen friend. What made me do this? How did I react so fast?

As I grew older, I rebelled against the hollow lives and lies of the "grown-ups" and turned into a juvenile delinquent, taking pleasure in seemingly minor affronts such as scaring old ladies by leaning out the window of a car and slapping hard on the side. Other people were totally unrelated to me, objects of scorn. By the age of fifteen, I was a member of a suburban, middle-class gang that drank to get drunk and engaged in random violence against persons and things. I puked so much I was known as "Mr. Puke." Twice I got into ferocious fights that I learned about only the next morning. This was not social drinking, which we despised as pretentious. Why did our disaffection with society turn to violence?

Near the end of the ninth grade, out of fear of the tedium of public school and of the reputation of a particularly aggressive teacher at the high school who treated students as inmates, I went for an interview at Pomfret School in Connecticut, where I was pleased to find myself treated as a human being: when the teacher who was showing me around the campus punched me playfully in the upper arm, I punched him back and he liked it! I enrolled, grateful to escape from the dreary confines of public school. During my senior year, in fourth-year Latin, the small group of us—most of us were avoiding taking chemistry—used to make fun of the alcoholic teacher, who looked ever so slightly like a pig, by oinking when he turned his back, and yet I underwent a most profound change of character watching and feeling how he explained the psychology of Virgil's *Aeneid*. Where did our lack of kindness come from?

I graduated first in my class, receiving a copy of Ovid's *Metamorphoses* as my prize, and entered Harvard in 1958. In college I gave up wrestling while recuperating from a cracked rib, even though in prep school I had reveled in humiliating opponents with a half nelson—the simplest of pins, but with power so crushing that my opponents couldn't breathe. But by this time, I just plain felt that I had conquered enough people; I didn't want to do it anymore. Something was starting to change my heart.

After my freshman year, inspired by Thoreau, I retreated to the woods of Vermont, where I went on long walks, came alive to colors, dreamt out all my bad dreams, and wrote poetry. I had found a part of the way toward filling the pit of loneliness and anger that had dominated my life. When the cold weather hit, motivated by Herman Melville's *Typee* and Somerset

Maugham's *The Moon and Sixpence*, I set out from New York on a freighter for Tahiti. After passing through the Panama Canal, I meditated on the sky for ten days, lying on the small top deck on the windward side of the smokestack, filling my mind with the marvelous blueness of that truly pacific ocean. When I reached Tahiti, I was astounded by the fact that the other runaways had no interest in discussing their own histories; they just wanted beer and a wahine, and indeed the latter would sleep with the rich, get some money, buy us beer at the sidewalk bar, sit on our laps, diddle with us right there, and occasionally spit out the tuberculosis sputum that plagued them. Eventually, the multicolored, flashing scenery of the island became like looking into a kaleidoscope all day long, and besides, the French imperialists found out I did not have a visa; so I left. This was not what I wanted. But what did I want?

Returning to college after a year and a half, I started drinking hard again. I have a dizzying memory of trying to stare at the wooden chair in front of me during my eleven o'clock Russian literature course. One night, a friend gave me a bottle of rum for reading Beat poetry at a Harvard club (where I was almost roughed up for reading Allen Ginsberg). After drinking most of it, I wandered up to Massachusetts Avenue, where I found myself faced by a glass doorway. I intended to break the bottle against the door, but the opposite happened: I swung the bottle, and the door shattered into pieces. Rushing back to my room, I fell facedown into bed, waking the next morning shaking from the fear of being arrested. But when it dawned on me that I was mimicking Raskolnikov in *Crime and*

Punishment, I laughed a little and started regaining some of my mental health. Where did these saving moments come from?

A year and a half later, in the summer between my junior and senior years, I retreated for six weeks to a cabin on a lake at North Hadley in Quebec Province. It was hard to get to. I went by canoe, navigating the three miles of choppy water by myself. When I started out, an old man had warned me I wouldn't make it, but I used my pack as ballast and rode perpendicular to the waves. The six weeks away gave my mind the time it needed to settle down. At the beginning I was so physically depleted I couldn't go for walks, especially since the cabin was on a steep hill, but in time I got stronger and stronger and would climb up the hill every day and meditate on the sky.

I spent the rest of summer vacation in Oklahoma near a river, where I continued my practice of lying on the ground staring at the sky. I used to float down The River, as it was called, in a tube. Sometimes I would get off my tube and stare at the water moving over the rocks; I saw that what I imagined as the river was water constantly changing and that there was no river like the one that I, or anyone else, was imagining. The ever-changing water prompted an experience much like one in childhood when, on my high chair at the dining room table, I would stare at a candle flame, seeing that it was always changing. I'd stare right into the center of it, and even though it always had a yellow color, it was always vibrating ever so slightly. There wasn't anything constant there that you could call the flame, as if it actually existed for some time. These childhood perceptions coupled with staring at the sky and now the river led me to realize that nothing remains. The stuff of ourselves is like the flame or the water. What existed a few moments ago is not somehow sitting on top of the present.

One day floating down The River, I saw an old man sitting on the bank, his head drooping to one side, who looked as if he had died. I suddenly realized that his last perception in this lifetime would be no fuller than any of his other perceptions. The accumulated perceptions of a lifetime did not go into the last perception to make it scintillating and rich and profound, but rather he merely would have looked to the side, much as anyone, and then died. Experiences are not like baggage; you don't fill up a suitcase with experiences and have them with you in palpable form. I began to recognize the ultimate futility of external activities, and to turn my attention inward to a light within.

When I returned to Harvard in the fall of 1962, it was as if a coffin had been opened; I had been living my life in a coffin and had not recognized the presence of sky. The Oklahoma sky meditation had developed to the point where, when I returned to the East, suddenly there was sky there too—my whole world opened up.

I had a single room on the seventh floor of Harvard's Leverett House that last year. It faced north with an ugly view, so I covered the bay window with junk plywood from boxcars at the lumberyard that my father managed and where I sometimes worked. I put a nature scene of geese on the covered window, and covered the wooden venetian swing-blinds over the smaller windows on each side with burlap at night so that the windows could be opened slightly but no light would enter the room. I made a rug for the ugly tile floor by sewing together burlap bags from the farm where my oldest brother was working, and with the same burlap I covered the crack between the door and the hall, thus producing a totally dark room for meditation. Total darkness is, in many ways, like infinite sky.

I would lie on my bed sometimes all night long without moving, through and beyond the excruciating pain that comes with utter lack of movement, to the point where the room became alive with hallucinations and all kinds of lights. Sometimes during the day I would do my sky meditation on the banks of the Charles River. One day the sky filled with little points of light; instead of conveying a sense of distance, the sky itself became quite sparkly and low.

I was getting overwhelmed with the fragility of mind brought on by these meditations on the sky and in total darkness and with developing a capacity to put my body to sleep immediately upon sitting down, reducing nervous activity so that my body was in a trancelike state. Hallucinating at will, I followed Jung's advice to use creative imagination and developed a relationship with an eagle that I imagined would fly into my room. But this exercise seemed useless and even counterproductive—I didn't want to be swallowed up by random imagination. I was looking for something else.

A close friend who wanted to help had heard about the Lamaist Buddhist Monastery of America (now the Tibetan Buddhist Learning Center) in New Jersey. We traveled there and saw Geshe Wangyal, a wily Kalmyk Mongolian adept-scholar who had studied in Tibet for thirty-five years. When he opened the door to his pink ranch house in the flatlands of New Jersey he revealed a Tibetan temple that filled the living room. I was flabbergasted. Never again would I assume that nothing was going on in the living rooms of America!

I didn't have much time with him and wasn't very impressed, but, for a reason I now do not remember, I came back for a second visit about a month later. I asked, "What is emptiness?" He teased, "You should know what *shunyata* [the Sanskrit word for emptiness] is. You are going to Harvard." But this failed to challenge me. Later in the conversation he said, "You won't be able to go into these topics seriously, but as you are going back and forth to work in Boston on the subway after you graduate, you can think about this." And he taught me a central Tibetan practice on how to develop compassion and altruism. It involves a series of meditations that build one on top of the other, culminating in a strong sense of empathy for all beings.

He talked about the foundational step of this series of meditations—the generation of equanimity, the practice of realizing on an intimate level how everyone has similar and basic aspirations to gain pleasure and get rid of pain. He spoke movingly about visualizing friends, enemies, and neutral people as equally wanting happiness and not wanting suffering. The realization of such equality is the foundation for cultivating compassion, which is the further wish that everyone be free from suffering and the causes of suffering. This preliminary exercise for generating equanimity really took hold of me when I returned to college. Meditating in my room, I would take to mind someone whom I knew. Instantly, my mind was racked either by desire, hatred, or jealousy—very obvious emotions. I felt, "This is my mind, I should be able to visualize people without these emotions overwhelming me," but I couldn't. I became fascinated by trying to conduct the meditation, thinking, "These are just appearances occurring to my mind, and I should be able to take these people to mind just as appearances." But I could not.

So I began methodically to meditate on people, going back through the course of my life. It was a matter of eventually going back to all my classrooms, where I was sitting among all my classmates, and thinking about each one: "This person wants happiness and doesn't want suffering just as I want happiness and don't want suffering." Doing this freed from autonomy the frozen experiences of my life, the fractured state of my mind. Memories of pleasant and unpleasant events in childhood were gradually reinstated. Eventually I was reconnected, reintegrated to the person who was crawling around as a baby. I had found what I was looking for—a powerfully beneficial technique to incrementally transform the mind into caring about others.

A month before my last exam, I was so taken by the mental transformation that was under way that I made the decision not to return to the woods to write poetry, as I had intended, but to enter the monastic life. Given that I had finished my course work in three and a half years and that my father would have to pay for the extra credits I had accumulated if I graduated, I decided to forgo graduating. Who needed a degree in a Buddhist monastery anyway! So, I moved to the monastery and I stayed for five years. Initially Geshe Wangyal had me get my books and then sent me back for my final exam (in geology). I graduated magna cum laude and received the Leverett prize for my translation of the Anglo-Saxon poem "The Wanderer." When the Leverett House master awarded my degree, he said (using my first name, Paul), "A modern-day Thoreau, a lover of nature, who travels alone through Canadian forests. A seeker after final truths, Paul is one of the most unusual and spiritually gifted men in his class." (Even now I am still inspired by Thoreau—though perhaps not so much by his individualism—and wander in woods, overwhelmed by the beauty of it all.)

At the monastery, I learned Tibetan and practiced forms of meditation that are known throughout the vast Tibetan cultural region, which stretches from Tibet itself through Kalmyk Mongolian areas where the Volga empties into the Caspian Sea (in Europe), to Outer and Inner Mongolia, to the Buriat Republic of Siberia, as well as to Ladakh, Sikkim, Bhutan, and much of Nepal. The meditations that form the structure of this book center around cultivating compassion and reflecting on the true nature of phenomena, and to this day they remain the heart of my daily practice.

The two years following my stay at the monastery were spent doing course work in the doctoral program of Buddhist Studies at the University of Wisconsin, after which I went to

India for dissertation research on a Fulbright. I quickly decided to go to Dharamsala, where the Dalai Lama lives, although I was specifically told by the director of the Fulbright Commission in New Delhi not to go there because of political sensitivities—which meant that the Chinese government insisted (and still does) that the Dalai Lama be isolated. By luck, two days later, the Dalai Lama began giving a series of sixteen lectures in Dharamsala for four to six hours each day on the stages of the path to enlightenment. Though I originally figured that a governmentally recognized reincarnation could not be very profound, I gradually became captivated by his insights to the point where I wrote several inspired poems of praise to him in Tibetan. Through a series of audiences, he took me on as his private student and eventually as his chief interpreter on ten tours from 1979 to 1989 in the United States, Canada, Malaysia, Singapore, Indonesia, Australia, Great Britain, and Switzerland. We collaborated in producing seven books, including *The Meaning of Life* (a bestseller in France). My life was immeasurably enriched through being so often in his compassionate presence and being faced with the intellectual demands that interaction with him requires.

Since starting my training, I have studied with eighteen Tibetan and Mongolian lamas, made ten trips to India and five to Tibet, published seventeen articles and twenty-three books in a total of twenty languages, done this and done that, but the thrust has always been to apply doctrine to practice and never to see doctrine as an end in itself. In this book, I want to share with you what insights I have gained from practicing techniques for cultivating compassion. I feel the topic is particularly relevant because, based on my own experience, I have learned that from the infection of an attitude of "me against the world"—when the bottom line is SELF, SELF, SELF—either despair or merciless competitiveness erupts, undermining one's own happiness as well as that of everyone around us, rending asunder the fabric of society, the very basis of a happy life. Without compassion, biting criticism of others is unchecked, eventually attacking in its own autonomous and random way even one's friends, one's family, one's own body, and oneself. Without compassion, politics becomes a matter of mere power blocks, counterproductively pushing other blocks around to the point where all interests are eventually thwarted. A compassionless perspective leads to the mania of thinking that mere economic success, while admittedly important, is the be-all and end-all of human existence; it gives rise to amoral and even immoral pursuit of money, in which one does not recognize the difference between adequate external facilities and true internal satisfaction.

The lessons and techniques presented here are especially useful because, as they are able to gradually transform an indifferent and even angry mind into one at least a little more caring and concerned, they offer up hope for a saddened world. Lately, some have declared that this millennium will see a trend toward compassion. May it be so! Since it is not enough to be told to be compassionate, the exercises offered in this book may be valuable; I certainly have found them so.

1

MEDITATION

HAVE YOU EVER NOTICED how difficult it is to keep track of your thoughts? The mind wanders so easily from the topic we want to keep it on. It even may seem that the mind is, in its own nature, like bubbles on a river or a ball floating in a stream. Actually, the nature of the mind is like water—not the bubbles or ripples on the surface or the movement but just the water itself. Nevertheless, because of our addiction to the superficial appearances of things, we feel that the mind naturally goes from one thing to another. It is as though we are in a bus and the driver takes us wherever she wants, at which point we decide that wherever we have arrived is a nice place to be. This is what makes it difficult to engage in practice like unbiased compassion that opposes the conditioned flow of the mind.

Since an attitude such as unbiased compassion, which runs against the grain of our usual outlook, is not easy, it has to be cultivated in meditation. Gradually, feeling develops, and then the felt attitude comes with only slight effort, and eventually it arises naturally and spontaneously. You practice in this way until compassion and altruism seem to form even the very stuff of your body.

It takes long meditation over months and years for new attitudes such as profoundly felt compassion to be sufficiently strong to remain of their own accord. Therefore, in the initial stages, the test of success is incremental progress, slight changes in daily behavior. Even with effective meditation, in which strong experience is gained during the session, it is easy—outside of the session—to fall back into old attitudes in the midst of daily activities.

Unskilled meditators, based on what is indeed an overpoweringly deep experience during a session of meditation, sometimes cannot face that they so easily fall back into old habits. Some even make the outrageous claim that the desire or the hatred that arises outside of or even during meditation is spiritually driven, somehow consistent with their new insights. However, the reversion to familiar patterns needs to be recognized as just what it is: we're used to our old ways and slip back into them, perhaps even more powerfully now that we have, through meditation, gained a more focused mind. Such reversion shows only that we need a sense of humor and more meditation.

The Tibetan word for meditation is *sgom pa* (pronounced "gom pa"). In a play on words, it's said that meditation (*sgom pa*) means familiarization (*goms pa*), both *s*'s being unpronounced. Thus, meditation means familiarize with, get used to, become a habit. You are seeking to regularize the practice so that it has a chance to affect everyday behavior, and to accomplish this, short periods of meditation are much better than long ones. The reason is that an intensity of purpose can be retained throughout a short session. When you do a long period of meditation without intensity, you're getting accustomed to—habituating yourself to—dullness. So, frequent short periods of cultivation are best.

There are very few people who have cultivated compassion so strongly in former lives that, when they sit down to cultivate it in this life, the meditation flows like a stream, with no obstruction at all. Even if we are drawn to the meditation, we extend compassion to our friends easily and to people toward whom we are neutral not so easily, but when we get to the people we dislike, the meditation becomes knotty. Essentially, we fake it. The only way it can become genuine and spontaneous is through training—through getting used to it. Part of developing familiarity is learning to realize as consciously as possible how the attitude we are cultivating seems to disagree with the present drift of our minds. If we merely placed a superficial overlay of thought on top of our actual feelings, we would not transform them but repress them. Repression doesn't work. What we avoid comes out in some other way and becomes the very thing that ruins the chance to make the perspective we are cultivating spontaneous. We have to face what we dislike. Often, however, we practice our dislikes so strongly that we cannot set them aside even for a moment. Many of us have a strained relationship with our parents, but there was a time when Mommy and Daddy were the greatest things in the whole universe. What keeps us from remembering them like that even for a few moments? The continual destructive thoughts that we habitually direct toward them.

Thus, it's important to keep in mind that developing compassion takes a tremendous amount of training of the mind with incremental progress. Although in meditation there are often sudden leaps to truly grand feelings, they are temporary. What is important over the long run is a steady progression. A good way to facilitate this progress is through discussing and sharing obstacles and successes with others. I often conduct group sessions in which I lead people through the series of meditations starting with equanimity and culminating in generating compassion. We do a particular exercise and then I'll ask, "What new feelings did you have?" From someone else's description of success, you may intuit how to break through a blockage about a person toward whom you can't even think, "That person wants happiness and doesn't want suffering." By hearing about and thus imagining another's success, it increases your own progress. If you are bored with trying to cultivate compassion toward people who are neutral to you—who have neither helped nor harmed you—it can be most helpful and inspiring to hear from another person who is having just the opposite experience: "Wow! It was amazing to extend the recognition of wanting happiness and not wanting suffering to so-and-so at work." Furthermore, when you, as a participant, talk about your own blocks, the very fact that you bring up a block as a difficult situation opens your mind to moving toward a solution. Talking out the obstacles usually doesn't remove them, but it does start a movement toward amelioration.

Occasionally you might even get stuck in a stupor and wonder, "What am I doing here? What is it I was doing?" It might take time for you to remember, "Oh, I was supposed to be cultivating compassion." Whenever you find that your mind has wandered, bring it gently back to the topic. Don't be ashamed, but also don't react with pride or fancy that somehow your mind decided that the meditation was not worthwhile and deliberately wandered either to another topic or into blankness. Just turn your mind back to the topic.

If you are worried about adding a regular practice to your already hectic routine, rest assured that meditating on compassion need not take up hours of your day. When I first went to Dharamsala, India, in 1972, the Dalai Lama was teaching the Stages of the Path to Enlightenment, and in the midst of the series of lectures he conducted a refuge ceremony that subsequently required all of us to take refuge in Buddha, his doctrine, and the spiritual community six times a day through thoughtful repetition of a formula: "I go for refuge to Buddha, his doctrine, and the spiritual community until I am enlightened. Through the merit of my charity, ethics, patience, effort, concentration, and wisdom, may I achieve Buddhahood for the sake of all beings." Initially I thought, "How can I *possibly* take refuge six times a day? I don't have enough time." However, refuge is very fast; it's ridiculous to think I wouldn't have time for it. Of course I had time for it. It's just that I wasn't used to it. It takes all of fifteen seconds. And six times—you could even do six in a row, and it would still only take a minute and a half! Anyone can find three minutes here and there throughout the day to practice compassion.

POSTURE

Meditation does not have to be done in a particular posture; it can and should be done in a variety of positions—standing, sitting, walking, riding on the bus, flying in a plane, wherever and whenever, provided you won't cause an accident. A change of position now and then helps to bring the force of the reflections into everyday life and deepen their impact. However, there is a particular sitting posture that, over the long run, can give a boost to the focus and staying power of meditative sessions.

This posture has seven features:

1. Sit on a comfortable cushion in either the lotus or the half-lotus posture, as they are sometimes called. In Tibet, they are called the vajra posture and the half-vajra posture. *Vajra* is a Sanskrit word meaning diamond, or diamond scepter, something unbreakable; the vajra posture is solid, indestructible. Though one can meditate in any posture at all, this specific sitting posture is recommended because of the heaviness of our afflictive emotions, including our tendency toward drowsiness; it is hard for the mind to be fully present when one is lying down, for example.

   The cushion should be comfortable. Preferably, there

should be two cushions: a large square cushion, as in Zen meditation, and on top of that, a smaller, either square or round cushion for the buttocks, which you may find more comfortable if it is quite hard; neither cushion should be very soft. The top one should be large enough so that the sides of the buttocks do not hang over but small enough so that the knees are on the bottom cushion.

In the half-vajra posture, the right leg is bent under the left; the left foot rests either near the groin, in the fold formed by the bending of the right leg, or on top of the right leg or the right thigh. Sitting in the half-vajra posture is a good technique for preparing to sit in the full vajra posture. You can start by putting the left foot on the right thigh, not in the fold at the groin. That gets the left knee and foot used to being bent. If you can't do that, sit with the left leg bent close to the body and the right leg extended in front, slightly bent. When I started, I could hardly bend my legs at all, but Geshe Wangyal made us sit while he taught us, almost all day long, on a floor that was covered only by a thin rug. After a while, it didn't make any difference how we sat; it was just painful.

The full-vajra posture begins from the half-vajra, but the right foot goes on top of the left thigh. Many people think that it is important to put both feet as close to the groin as possible. One of my lamas told me that there was no benefit in this at all, that it is much better to sit more loosely—to bring the left leg out more and set the right foot almost at the knee. Some sit with both feet close to the groin, but if you can sit a half hour that way, you can sit an hour or two hours in this looser posture.

The lotus, or vajra, posture is solid and becomes comfortable in time. After several weeks or months, you will notice that both knees are resting on the lower cushion, but usually when starting this practice, your right knee is hanging in the air. One virtue of putting a cushion under the buttocks is that it allows both knees eventually to touch the floor. Keep in mind that this does not mean that your back is leaning forward. In contrast, if you sit on a level surface, the right knee will always tend to hang in the air.

There are various ways of dealing with discomfort in sitting. If the posture becomes painful, discontinue it. Uncross your legs immediately, massage the places that hurt, and get back into the posture at once. You'll see that this helps. I know a big man who was determined to stay in the vajra posture and broke his leg. You have to be careful and know when your body has to stop.

2. When seated on a comfortable cushion in the vajra or half-vajra posture, close your eyes, but not entirely. By closing your eyes at the start of a session, you can visualize much more easily. Your mind seems clearer, but in a short time it becomes duller than it would have been if you had faced the difficulty of keeping your eyes slightly open at the beginning—neither wide open nor closed, but aimed at the tip of the nose or, if that is uncomfortable, at the ground about a yard in front of you. The point, of course, is not to stare at the

tip of your nose but to set the eyes there so that you won't
be distracted by visual consciousness even though light will
still come to your eyes.

3. Straighten the body and spine and keep them straight. I
usually start by leaning forward a little and then straighten
back up. This stretches the fat of the buttocks so that, when
I straighten up again, the fat stays back and supports the
body, like a cushion, making it easier to sit straight. Otherwise, that fat is rolled underneath; you haven't stretched it,
and it acts as a counterforce to your staying upright.

4. Keep the shoulders level. You may need a friend to tell you
whether you are succeeding. Straighten them and cultivate
that feeling of straightness.

5. Keep the head even, with the nose in line with the navel.
Keeping the nose in line with the navel means not turning
your head. The head is not tilted back or forward, right or
left, but is not held quite level. Draw the neck back and bend
the head down a little, as a peacock does. You may wonder
how you can straighten your chest, stretch the back of your
head up, and bend the front of your head down at the same
time, but try it and you'll see why the comparison with a
peacock's head is made.

6. Set the teeth normally, with the tongue against the ridge
behind the upper teeth. This is to keep too much saliva from

flowing. Saliva is a problem in meditating. When I meditate with a group of people, I hear people swallowing a lot. Almost all systems of yoga say that it is important to breathe through your nose; therefore, keep your mouth closed and break any habit you may have of breathing through your mouth.

7. Breathe quietly and gently. It is terrible when you sit down to meditate with a group of people and there are people in the group who feel they're supposed to breathe audibly. If you breathe audibly, you'll distract any companions you may be meditating with. It is also bad for you, because the mind is overpowered by the movement of the breath; you can even become dizzy after a while through breathing so hard. The point is to breathe so gently that you yourself do not hear it. Bear in mind that beginners should not force themselves to breathe extremely slowly or to retain the breath.

To recap the seven features:
1. Sit on a cushion in the vajra or half-vajra posture.
2. Keep the eyes partly closed and aimed at the point of the nose.
3. Keep the body and spine straight.
4. Keep the shoulders level.
5. Keep the head even, bent down a little, the nose in line with the navel.
6. Set the teeth normally, with the tongue against the ridge behind the upper teeth.
7. Breathe quietly and gently.

One of the main reasons for this posture is that the mind is said to ride on the breath—or what are called winds, currents of energy. This posture straightens the channels through which these energies course, thereby straightening the energies and thus the mind, which then tends to abide in its natural state.

What do you do with your hands? There are many positions. One is to press gently with the thumb of each hand at the base of the ring finger of the same hand; this has an effect on the energies that serve as the basis for afflictive emotions. Or place your hands on your knees. Or put your left palm upward in the lap and place the right hand on top of it, palm downward. This position concentrates energies together. Or place the left hand in the lap, palm upward, and the right hand on top of it, palm upward. Or simply rest your hands in your lap. Or put your hands flat on the floor and lean back for a while. This posture revivifies a tired mind.

The mind can become steady in meditation, but if it does not remain brilliantly on its object, that steadiness becomes a subtle kind of laxity, which is an obstacle to *intense* clarity. The various aspects of the physical posture assist in attaining prolonged, intense clarity.

STEPS IN CULTIVATING COMPASSION

Compassion cannot be accomplished all in one session. Before you begin, it helps to get an overview of the several steps involved in developing deep and continuous compassion.

The overview itself exerts an influence on the mind, drawing it toward the ultimate state being sought. Here's a chapter-by-chapter outline of the six-step process, along with several booster meditations:

Chapter 2

1. The foundational step of equanimity—realizing that everyone wants happiness and does not want suffering; cultivation of equanimity is bolstered by the series of eight meditations:

Chapter 3

+ How to empower practice by adjusting your motivation beforehand and by dedicating its value afterward

Chapter 4

+ How to become more realistic by meditating on the nearness of death
+ How to develop a strong intention to utilize the precious opportunity of this life
+ How to lessen the force of previous negative actions through a four-step technique: disclosure of ill deeds, contrition, intention of restraint in the future, and virtuous activity

Chapter 5

+ How to remove barriers to equanimity and compassion through a three-phase technique: imagination of hell-like situations, relieving those beings of pain, and reflecting on

the similarity of aspiration between yourself and them
+ How to transform reactions by remembering conflict situations earlier in your life and imagining a change of attitude
+ How to overcome fright by imagining dream-monsters and contemplating that the monster, like you, wants to be rid of suffering and gain happiness

Chapter 6
+ How to cultivate equanimity by imagining specific relationships in past lifetimes

Chapter 7
2. Meditating on everyone as close, using your best friend as the model; enhancements are presented in the next two chapters:

Chapter 8
+ How to proceed effectively and remove obstacles

Chapter 9
+ How to separate from selfishness by choosing who should be helped, by radiating beneficence to them, and by enjoying others' success

Chapter 10
3. Reflecting on the kindness of individuals, intended and unintended

Chapter 11

4. Developing a determination to reciprocate kindness

Chapter 12

5. Meditating three levels of love

Chapter 13

6. An overview of the three levels of compassion, described in the next three chapters, as well as enhancement by wisdom, described in the final chapter:

Chapter 14

✦ Cultivating compassion seeing suffering beings through contemplating the example of a bucket battered in a well

Chapter 15

✦ Cultivating compassion seeing evanescent beings through contemplating the example of the reflection of the moon in a rippling lake

Chapter 16

✦ Cultivating compassion seeing empty beings through contemplating the example of the reflection of the moon in a calm lake

Chapter 17

✦ Compassion and wisdom affecting each other

These chapters present techniques for gradually generating heartfelt compassion by removing obstacles and opening the mind to the sensibleness of care and concern for others. Encapsulations of instructions for meditation are in bold type so that they are easily utilized in practice sessions.

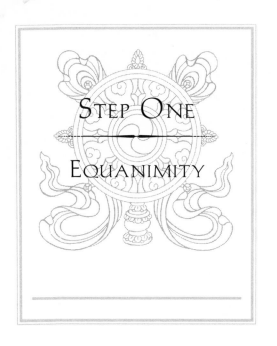

STEP ONE

EQUANIMITY

EQUALITY

DURING A LECTURE while I was interpreting for the Dalai Lama, he said in what seemed to me to be broken English, "Kindness is society." That's a strange thing to say. At the time, I wasn't smart enough to think he was saying kindness *is* society. I thought he meant kindness is important *to* society, kindness is *vital to* society. But he was saying that kindness is so important that we cannot have society without it. Society is impossible without it. Thus, kindness IS society; society IS kindness. It's impossible to have society without concern for other people. We've experimented for a century or more to see if we could have society without kindness, and the decision has finally been reached that *it don't work.*

Both capitalist countries and communist countries have given a try to see if we could have society without kindness, based on some other principle such as oneself first or the state first. The state—as the latter folks saw it—is not society but some entity beyond society, whatever that could possibly be.

Both approaches—unbridled capitalism and communism—
have been miserable failures. Controlling people through coer-
cion doesn't work, whatever the technique. Whatever coercive
method the government works out, the other side will get
around it. For instance, if the government develops an eaves-
dropping system to control what somebody is doing in the
next room, that person will work out a counter system that
blocks it. Then, the feds devise a more sophisticated one that
penetrates the wall so they can see what's going on, and the
people in the next room figure out a way to jam that system.
The adversarial cycle goes on and on. As long as the spirit of
cooperation, the spirit of wanting to take care of one another, is
not there, it is impossible to devise a workable system.

The Dalai Lama is fond of saying, when beginning to address
a group on a lecture tour, that he feels he knows each individual just like his own brother or sister—even though he's of a
different religion than most of the people who are listening
to him, and was brought up in a different part of the world,
speaks a different language, and wears different clothes. But
his basic knowledge of himself provides knowledge of what
all beings want.

Actually, we all know each other quite well. Sometimes,
when the Dalai Lama says that we all want happiness and do
not want suffering, this seems to be a platitude, not worth saying. But it *is* worth saying, contemplating, and making into a
meditation, because we *don't* remain in constant recognition
that just as *I* want happiness and don't want suffering, so *you*
want happiness and don't want suffering. Rather, we might

think, "Oh, yes, I want happiness and don't want suffering, and yes, these people want happiness and don't want suffering. Yes, of course." But all too often our next thought is, "How can they serve me?"

My usual habits draw me into thinking, "How can you serve my quest for pleasure and my quest to get rid of pain?" However, if I remember that I want happiness and don't want suffering and you equally have the same aspiration, I cannot possibly ask you to serve me. If gaining happiness and getting rid of suffering are worthwhile for me, then they're worthwhile for everyone equally.

SEEING ONLY WITH OUR EYES

Since I first noticed my unwillingness to live in constant recognition of this basic quality of all sentient beings—not just humans but also animals—I've tried to think about what prevents such constant recognition. We're all so similar, yet somehow it's so easy to cross that line and use other people for one's own happiness—in ways we would never want to be used ourselves. Far from making myself available for others' happiness, everyone else—no matter how large the number—should be available, from my point of view, for my happiness. If you don't contribute to my happiness, watch out!

What is it about our minds that keeps us from this recognition, that makes it so easy to forget? One factor is that we mainly encounter others through the medium of sight—through our visual consciousness, our eyes. We mainly *see* other people, but we mainly *feel* ourselves and remain primarily concerned with our own feelings of warmth, cold, hunger, thirst, breathing, having this pleasure or that pain. We use radically different modes for self and other.

Because we so often use the medium of sight to form our knowledge of others, we see persons in silly categories such as black, white, yellow, and red. In Tibetan monastic education, one of the first things that young monastics are asked in the debating courtyards is "Is a white horse white?" The proper answer is "No, the *color* of a white horse is white." A horse, like a human, is a sentient being, a person, and persons are not colors. We say so-and-so is black, and so-and-so is white, but these descriptions are totally inaccurate. Colors are merely material. Persons are designated in dependence upon mind and body, but they are neither mind nor body, nor even a collection of the two.

What we see as other people is merely color and shape. For us, that's the main basis for defining other people. We define ourselves, however, through feeling, and it is crucial whether that feeling is pleasurable or painful. We're seeking pleasure, seeking to get rid of pain, so we're in close touch with our own quest to gain happiness and remove suffering. With other people, since the main medium of perception is different, we tend to be less aware.

When I understood this, I realized why, when he went to Europe for the first time (I was not the translator for this trip but read news accounts), the Dalai Lama would arrive at a city and announce, "Everyone wants happiness and doesn't want suffering." In India I had attended long lectures by him—four to six hours a day, sixteen days running—on complicated philosophy and psychology, but when he came to Europe, what did he have to say? "Everyone wants happiness, doesn't want suffering." He would come to the airport and announce that everyone wants happiness, doesn't want suffering. He'd have a news conference in the city and announce that everyone wants happiness, doesn't want suffering. In city after city after city. I thought, "What's wrong with him?" It caused me to wonder if it was even relevant. *But it is relevant!* For understanding that others are so much like oneself creates a different perspective, a startlingly changed worldview. When this view is internalized, you are no longer confronting another person over a divide, but meeting someone with whom you have much in common. You begin to feel you know the person. Indeed, you begin to feel you know everyone.

One of the marvelous advantages I accrued from traveling with the Dalai Lama as his chief English interpreter for ten years was that he usually gave the first part of a talk in English, and thus I could hear his message over and over again. Though I heard it thousands of times, "Everyone wants happiness, doesn't want suffering," rather than boring me it would draw me again into thinking, "Yes, I need to internalize this attitude." I understood that on a personal, practical level I had to bring this orientation into moment-by-moment behavior. When you have a headache and want to get rid of it, imagine it's the same for everyone. There isn't anyone who deliberately wants more headache.

Meditation: Finding a Common Ground with
Everyone—Equanimity

Our habit-patterns are such that sometimes, when we see a person who is suffering, it generates happiness: "He's getting what he deserves!" Thus, in order to change your attitude— that is, if you decide that compassion is worth cultivating— most of us first have to find out *how* to change it. It is obvious that if a friend suffers, we are unhappy, but if an enemy suffers, we feel joy. Toward those who are neutral, we are indifferent; if we read that someone we don't know is in the hospital or has died, we pass on to the next topic. But if we are to generate great compassion, equal compassion for every being, it is necessary to see *all* beings as close—as close and dear as our own best friend. To do this, it is first necessary to see that all beings in certain respects are equal. Living in a big city, sometimes we feel that we don't know our neighbors and so forth, but actually we know them well. They want pleasure and don't want pain. This realization of similarity is not superficial, such as knowing that each of us has hairs in the nose and thus we can always know something about others by reflecting on the fact that everybody has hairs in the nose. This may be a meaningful reflection, but it is not central, as is the fact that we all want happiness and don't want suffering. When we meditatively cultivate this reflection that we all want happiness, the way we interact with other people changes.

This being the case, the first step in cultivating compassion is simply to contemplate people whom you know, starting with friends, then neutral people, and gradually work with enemies. **In meditation, contemplate: "Just as I want happiness and don't want suffering, this person wants happiness and doesn't want suffering."** This preparatory meditation is called equanimity, or evenmindedness, in that you are learning to place at the core of your relationships with others the deeply felt realization that everyone *equally* aspires to gain happiness and to be rid of suffering.

It's important to stress the equality between oneself and others. It isn't sufficient to think superficially: "Just as I want happiness, don't want suffering, this person wants happiness, doesn't want suffering; and that person wants happiness, doesn't want suffering." You would not bring home the point that there is equality between this person and that person, between this person and a third person, and between this other person and a fourth person.

Therefore, when you reflect on the first part, "Just as I want happiness," *feel* it. Then *feel* "and don't want suffering." Then extend it to someone else: "so this person wants happiness, doesn't want suffering." By proceeding this way, you will establish an orientation around feeling—you will understand the primary feeling—orientation of the other person, whereby the other person becomes on a par with yourself. This quality of parity is crucial. It doesn't wipe out other differences, but it is vitally important and can be transformative in your life.

It is not sufficient to make just one grand gesture, because later when there's trouble with a particular person, you have no memory of the gesture at all. You can easily end up thinking, "May all sentient beings be happy; just as I want happiness and don't want suffering, so *all* sentient beings want happiness and don't want suffering—but you better get out of my way!"

For this reason, it is necessary to meditate specifically, person by person. If in your meditation you thought everybody was neutral over the course of a lifetime, then everybody was a friend, and finally everybody at some point was an enemy, that "everybody" would be too vague. The result would be that when somebody is nasty to you, it wouldn't apply. It may help a little, but it won't apply in specific situations. So, start with easier persons—friends and neutral persons—and then proceed to harder ones: minor enemies, and so forth. You have to really feel the pain of others and gain familiarization with the meditation to the point where it has impact.

Naturally, this process takes time. Also a sense of humor, a delight in watching how hard it is to apply this simple principle to some people. "Just as I want happiness and don't want suffering, so the woman sitting next to me on the airplane wants happiness and doesn't want suffering—the woman who kept waking me up!" Go through all the people in the plane, one by one: "The pilot wants happiness and doesn't want suffering . . ." Meditate on people at work you don't really know, people in a pharmacy—it's shocking to recognize their humanity— the pharmacist behind the counter whom you've seen several times but you only recognize: ". . . she wants happiness and doesn't want suffering. . ." This simple thought can translate into WOW!

It is often recommended to begin this exercise with neutral people and then to pass on to those whom you like, because you can get too involved with other thoughts about your friends. Still, because it's easy to recognize that your friends want happiness and don't want suffering, you can get a measure of what it's like for this attitude of self-other equality to awaken and to come home to you by considering your friends first. As you go down a list of friends, you will probably notice that as you reflect on each of them, you have stronger and weaker wishes for their well-being.

As you cultivate this attitude more and more, it can become more and more shocking, even with respect to neutral people. "Whew! All those neutral people want happiness, don't want suffering? All those people on the street?" Meditate wherever you are. All persons, this person, that person, they all want happiness. It's hard to repeat because there are a lot of words and you can easily turn what can be highly evocative emotionally into just sounds and syllables. Nevertheless, keep repeating the whole message: "Just as I want happiness, don't want suffering, so Francis wants happiness, doesn't want suffering. So my neighbor Frank wants happiness, doesn't want suffering." And so on.

Don't shy away from reflecting on strangers. "This person pulling the weight-machine bars down wants happiness, doesn't want suffering." Interesting! "The guy leaning against the windows at the gym wants happiness, doesn't want suffering." So, too, the persons who take our identification cards as we come into the gym also want happiness, don't want suffering. Getting used to this process and passing through the shock again and again is provocative, transforming. It makes you see the world in a whole new light. It is more than just a truism.

Many years ago when I was lecturing in Pennsylvania, a woman asked me, "Why are you talking so much about becoming compassionate and so forth? Just be yourself." I said, "That might work for you. Maybe that's what you would do, but were it not for my efforts to cultivate compassion, I would mainly seek to take care of myself. Even at the expense of others. I need a transformative technique."

Once you have experienced this equanimity with respect to individual people, first a few friends and then neutral people, then, and only then, carry it over to enemies: those who have harmed, are harming, or will harm you or your friends. Don't start with your worst enemies; start with your least enemies. "Just as I want happiness and don't want suffering, so does so-and-so, that son of a bitch, want happiness and not want suffering." No, no, no, no, no! Let go of the resistance that you feel.

When the government wants to bomb somebody like Saddam Hussein, they first make him into a mad dog. They dehumanize him, separate him from the rest of us. Then we feel it's okay to go ahead and bomb. This person is not really human; this person is not like me. So it's all right for me to do whatever I want to him or her. But when you've done the exercise enough so that you're not that easily diverted, even though these thoughts may appear, you recognize that it's not sensible. When this person has a headache, son of a bitch that he is, he must want to get rid of it, right? You have to admit it. Just as I want happiness and don't want suffering, so he wants happiness and doesn't want suffering.

We're conditioned to self-cherishing, to cherishing ourselves and our way of relating to others in particular situations. We do what we're used to, and we're not used to thinking about other people as wanting happiness and not wanting suffering. There will be many situations in which you find it hard to extend this recognition, such as when someone verbally attacks you—"You did it! If it weren't for you, everything would have gone all right." We often resist the recognition of equanimity because this person is so very happy exerting control.

But equanimity does not mean that you consider others' *ways* of getting happiness suitable and thus affirm them. Quite the opposite: you become more astute at not affirming them. The fact that the other person wants control is pathetic, isn't it? People have different estimations of what happiness is, and quite different estimations about how to achieve it. They use whatever smarts they have to determine the best techniques to bring it about, and often use some pretty silly means to achieve that end. From the viewpoint that this person wants control, she may not be like yourself, but in a very important sense, this person *is* like yourself. She wants happiness and doesn't want suffering. That she may be going about it blindly should make you feel compassion for her, rather than creating a reason to separate yourself further apart.

How awful it is that what she wants and what she is engaged in are at cross-purposes! She wants happiness and doesn't want suffering but is engaging in the causes of suffering. Isn't it sad? The person's blind adherence to a certain way of trying to become fulfilled becomes a reason for feeling closer. Easy to say, isn't it?

When we think so-and-so is a real jerk, we must also bring ourselves into the equation by remembering to do this exercise. It brings about an inclusion. When you see someone who is ruining the environment or acting badly on the job, you may feel very aggravated, but when you recall this basic similarity, it can be a shock. Consider political leaders that we find so easy to dislike. Who are the favorite politicians to hate? Who are some of your worst enemies? What about drug pushers hooking young people? Once the experience of equanimity is cultivated, there is no way to separate these individuals out from the class of humans by calling them scum. Without such a perspective, however, that's just what we are prone to do. When we label them scum, it makes it all right to do with them whatever we want: we don't fund needle exchanges for the drug pushers or other programs for them because these are sub-people, not within the count of humans. But remember: Just as I want happiness and don't want suffering, so do these people who have their own ideas of what happiness is. Such types of persons are too hard to start with—one might think about equanimity but not feel it. When you've cultivated this realization with respect to friends and neutral people and have experienced the shock of discovering this closeness, *then* you can work on developing this same sense of closeness to lesser enemies and finally to great enemies.

Equanimity—recognizing the equality of aspiration to happiness and to get rid of suffering—is the basis for love, compassion, and kindness. The appeal of the practice of equanimity and the subsequent exercises is to feeling—heart—not to abstract principles. Nor is there an appeal to "Buddha said so." The ground to work from is natural feelings. It's merely our nature that we want pleasure and do not want pain; no other validation is needed. It may seem like an abstract principle, but we live from within aspirations to happiness and avoidance of suffering all day long.

In the Buddhist perspective, it's not somebody else or some other being who made us this way—wanting happiness, not wanting suffering—that's how we are. Fire is hot and burning, that's the way it is. Who made it that way? It's the way it is. This is called the reasoning of nature. It's just the nature of things. It's our nature to want happiness and not want suffering, and thus Buddhists do not ask that one give up the pursuit of happiness but merely suggest that one become more intelligent about how it is pursued.

MOTIVATION

ADJUSTING YOUR MOTIVATION BEFORE PRACTICE

AT TIBETAN CEREMONIES and lectures, a formal part at the start is to adjust one's motivation. The assumption is that the motivation brought to the activity is not as wide as it could be. Most likely, it's not counterproductive, involving emotions such as lust or anger, but is just neutral. However, virtuous activity such as attending a religious ceremony or engaging in meditation should be initiated with a virtuous motivation, the ideal being to direct the motivation toward the benefit of other beings. When you start a session— whether on a cushion, on a chair, or walking about—you are apt to have been previously thinking within a narrow range, and thus your motivation has to be adjusted before you begin the practice. Thus it's important at the beginning of a session of any type of meditation to direct the value of performing the meditation to the welfare of sentient beings.

There's magic when, before beginning a meditation, you

extend the field of your motivation to many beings—as long as many individual beings appear to mind—because then the session will be connected to not just one small being, yourself, but with many, many others. As a result, its power will increase proportionately. The process of learning how to direct your motivation at the beginning of a session by patiently directing its value to individual persons requires time and practice for the implications to be brought home. **In meditation, do this by taking just one person to mind and thinking, "I am beginning this session of meditation for your sake."** When you experience a feeling extending out to that person, take to mind another person and repeat the process. Do this with at least ten persons at the start of each session. Gradually the field of your activity will grow and grow.

Start with people nearby. Don't make your altruistic intention so diffuse that it has no meaning, but slowly extend it on to your state or province and then to countries—to the United States, to Canada, Mexico, South America, Australia, China, Tibet, the Middle East, Africa, Eastern Europe, Western Europe, and so forth. If it becomes weak, come back and dedicate the value again to a smaller group, a few individuals, and then add, "by extension everyone else."

If the field is "all sentient beings," and it's not many *individual* beings, the referent is apt to be merely vague, and the meditation does not have much force. When any individual appears to your mind, your compassionate endeavor should be for that person too. Only after this is it possible to extend the altruistic motivation to groups such that the session is for them. Then when you've directed altruism to so many individuals and groups, "all" comes to have some meaning. Otherwise, saying "all" tends to mean "no one," and whenever anyone appears to your mind they aren't included in "all sentient beings" whereas, of course, they should be.

Then, whether meditating alone or with someone else or in a larger group, reflect that what you are doing—no matter how insignificant you might think its force is—is to benefit the entire world. It's evocative to consider that a thoughtful activity in a particular place can be tied into the whole cosmos such that even if the session doesn't produce much insight, the motivation with which you started is so powerful that it will still make a difference. Guaranteed success.

DEDICATING THE VALUE
OF A SESSION AFTER PRACTICE

At the end of a meditative session it's important to dedicate its value to the welfare of all sentient beings. **As you bring your session to a close, first consider individual people: "Whatever value there was in the meditation done here, may it be for the benefit of this person, that person. . ."** Imagine the people and the animals around you. Relating the activity to so many beings is a powerful way of increasing the force of what was a small virtuous activity. It's magically effective to picture that you did something for the people and animals you were contemplating as wanting happiness and not wanting suffering. As with adjusting the motivation at the beginning of the session, larger groups of individuals and communities can be considered later.

Start with the beings who are right with you in the room or nearby. When I meditate in a group, I dedicate the value I got out of the session—that intangible transformative force—to the persons in that group. "May it go to help each one of you." And then some of the beings around us. Don't let the field of dedication be vague, like "everyone," because then it disappears from the mind. Dedicate it to the meditators around you, and make sure to include the individual beings who were part of your reflections during the session.

Dedicating the value is like having $1,000 and giving $1,000 to each of the many persons I took to mind. I wouldn't be dividing it among them but giving each the full $1,000. Even more so is the case of the advantageous force of a session—in terms of my own happiness, and so forth, the session can do much more than money. What is it that brings us good luck? What is it that brings us good fortune? What is it that's brought us into this kind of lifetime? To give this intangible but powerful force, to dedicate *that* to other people, is to give the *best* thing that you have.

Dedication of the value of a session to many persons multiplies its force, because without such an attitude, the activity of meditation is related with just one person. But when you mentally dedicate it to, say, ten people, it's magnified ten times. So, though you give it away, you benefit. And, indeed, such generosity would certainly have an effect on how you act with other people. But also, and more importantly, on an immaterial level, it benefits others directly. Although often a solo practice, meditation can be very social.

Nagarjuna, a great Indian scholar-yogi who lived approximately six hundred years after the Buddha, speaks about the fact that since enlightenment is limitless, the causes of enlightenment have to be limitless also. He says not to worry about having to accumulate such a vast number of causes, since we can relate whatever virtuous practices we do to all beings. In the *Precious Garland*, speaking about bodhisattvas—those altruistically seeking to become enlightened—he says:

Do not feel inadequate about this [accumulation]
Of merit to achieve enlightenment,
Since reasoning and scripture
Can restore one's spirits.

Just as in all directions
Space, earth, water, fire, and wind
Are without limit,
So suffering sentient beings are limitless.

Through their compassion
Bodhisattvas are determined to lead
These limitless sentient beings out of suffering
And establish them in Buddhahood.

[Hence] whether sleeping or not sleeping,
After thoroughly assuming [such compassion]

Those who remain steadfast—
Even though they might not be meticulous—

Always accumulate merit as limitless as all sentient
   beings
Since sentient beings are limitless.
Know then that since [the causes] are limitless,
Limitless Buddhahood is not hard to attain.

[Bodhisattvas] stay for a limitless time [in the world];
For limitless embodied beings they seek
The limitless [good qualities of] enlightenment
And perform limitless virtuous actions.

Hence though enlightenment is limitless,
How could they not attain it
With these four limitless collections
Without being delayed for long?

Adjusting your motivation before practice ensures that it
will be much more powerful, more effective. Dedication at the
end of practice ensures that its impact will not be lost.

AWARENESS OF DEATH

T O GENERATE COMPASSION it is essential to know, to feel, how fragile others' lives are, how they are beset by suffering no matter who they are. And to know this, first it is necessary to realize how fragile your own life is—to stare your own suffering in the face. The fundamental suffering is death; being aware of it puts everything else into perspective.

Meditation:
Death Is Definite, But the Time Is Unsure
It is definite that one is going to die, and at the time of death and beyond, what is helpful are the mental predispositions that are carried from this lifetime to the next. Everything else at that point is of little help. I can't take my nice home in Virginia with me, nor my money, nor all sorts of accumulations, even friends. Even my body. At that point I will cast off my body or, from another point of view, it will cast off me. That which you took care of for so long, as if it were going to last at least a thousand years, ditches you.

It is definite that we are going to die, but it is not certain *when* we are going to die. One can die at any time—with even the young dying before the old, the well dying before the sick. The actuarial tables say that males as a whole will live so many years and females as a whole will live so many more years, but such figures are irrelevant with respect to any specific individual; if you're going to die next week, it's a hundred percent chance you're going to die then. It's not a such and such percentage that you might live to be seventy-eight. If you are to die on the road today, it's a hundred percent certain you'll die on the road today.

In order to value the time we have—to cherish it—it is important to reflect on the certainty of death and the uncertainty of when death will be. **In meditation, contemplate: "I will definitely die—as will all of us—but I don't know when I'm going to die. It could be at any time!"** Such reflection puts a value—a premium—on the present, on the time you have.

Meditation:

Making Use of the Precious Present Opportunity

Since it is obvious that the body and possessions are left behind, one needs to put more emphasis on consciousness. The predispositions that we carry within our minds are the crucial sources of help and harm. "Karma" has basically two elements: one is action—that is to say, physical, verbal, and mental actions themselves—and the other is the potencies, established by these actions, in the mind. They are like etchings or infusions of future tendencies that draw us into attitudes and situations. Thus "good karma" refers either to beneficial actions themselves or to favorable predispositions established by those actions. So, it's karma that matters, it's karma that shapes the future.

As much as karma has shaped the present, so it will shape the future. There is a famous Tibetan saying: "If you want to know what you were doing in the past, look at your body and present situation, because it was shaped by past actions. If you want to know what your situation will be in the future, look at what you're doing with your mind now." All pleasurable and painful feelings themselves are said to arise from karma, one's own previous actions. However slight the pain, however slight the pleasure, it's due to previous karma. This idea plays out every day when several of us are in the same situation, such as standing in the midst of a cool breeze, but it is not experienced by all the same way.

That the present is so much determined by our past actions seems deterministic, but, in another way, since karma means "doing," it's an indication that we can shape our own future through directing our motivation. Far from being deterministic, there's a good deal of free will. In fact, in Buddhist doctrines humans are said to have more will than other beings. Animals, for instance, do not accumulate the force of karma that humans do, because humans can put the force of intention behind their actions. Thus the doctrine of karma is a call to take responsibility for one's own future, to see that one's own situation is set up by one's own past karma, not somebody else's, and to use that knowledge to shape the road ahead.

The main source of our condition is to be attributed not to a separate "society" but to our own former actions. Buddhism is vastly different from much thought nowadays, in which society is blamed as the central debilitating factor. The frequent attitude is, "If we could only adjust society a little, everything would be fine." It does help to fix social structures, but a good part of the blame for our misfortunes belongs with us as individuals. Thus, Buddhism emphasizes the influence of our past actions, not for the sake of decreasing our sense of will—our sense that we have some power to choose our activities—but for the sake of showing the importance of the deeds we choose to do, since they have great influence on our future. Therefore, the doctrine of karma is not a call to lay aside effort and will; it is a call to make effort and use will. We are shaping our own paths.

Therefore, if you feel that you are mentally slower than others, don't simply accept it as your lot—employ a technique to get smarter. Ask many questions of others or keep a dictionary near you to look up words. Light candles or lamps to gods of wisdom, like Manjushri, the Buddhist incarnation of the wisdom of all Buddhas, or recite Manjushri's mantra, *om a ra pa ja na dhi,* saying it many, many times and at the end, repeating *dhi, dhi, dhi, dhi, dhi, dhi, dhi, dhi, dhi, dhi* as many times as you can.

As long as you are alive, something can be done to improve your current situation. Who can say with certainty that the old die before the young, or that the sick die before the well? With two other professors, I went to visit a very rich, aged professor who was bedridden with gout, cancer of the ganglia, a heart condition, and diabetes. We wanted to ask him for funds for our Center for South Asian Studies at the university, but when we were ushered into his bedroom and saw him lying so pathetically in a hospital bed, we merely paid our respects and left. As we were walking down his drive, I remembered this teaching and said, "We do not know who will die first— him or one of us." They were stunned, and as it turned out, the younger brother of one of the professors died before the aged professor who was ravaged with illness.

In meditation, contemplate: "Since death is definite and it's uncertain when I will die, I must make use of this precious opportunity of a human lifetime right now." One must take advantage of this rare opportunity and accumulate beneficial karma. The basic determinants are not money, or social position, but actions.

It's not that all of these many karmas get pooled in the mind into a blended mixture; they remain individual though many can manifest together like different colors in a painting. Some are activated at present, and some are not. One's own will, one's own wish, has a great deal to do with which karmas are activated and which ones are not.

Think of rebirth in the cycle of lives—or parts of one life—in which you were born, grew old, became sick, and died over and over in many different situations. There isn't any karma, any action, that you haven't done (consciously or unconsciously) in the past. Those predispositions reside with the mind.

One type of karmic effect is causally concordant in the sense that you do the same thing again. There's a concordance between what you did before and what you do now; your past actions have conditioned you to do the same now—habit.

Another type of karmic effect is that the action you did to someone else happens to you. Killing, and then being killed. Harming, and then being harmed. One lama painted a frightful picture of some marriages, saying that the karma could be such that you put yourself in a situation where you can harm each other easily. And the same with children; indeed, children can harm their parents very easily. Because you harmed that person in the past, the child is put into a situation where he or she can harm you easily. It's frightful. Looked at this way, this sort of cyclic existence is disgusting.

A third type of karmic effect is called environmental, because one is impelled into physical surroundings that correspond to one's actions. For instance, creating dissension between people, and then being born in a rocky, dry area where it's difficult to grow anything.

The last type of effect is called fruitional, because it impels a whole new lifetime. For those who do not have an inkling that rebirth is possible, this could be reframed as a life-altering experience.

In these four ways, what we do creates future events—by us and to us. The flexibility of effect suggests that on a deeper level, "self" and "other" do not mean as much as we often think they do. For example, we all know that in dreams self and other switch very easily. Sometimes we are pursued by beings who are manifestations of our own nasty thoughts. Our own actions shape both what we are in the future and what happens to us. Therefore, we need to pay particular attention to our actions, and since the force of karma is shaped by our intentions, we need to put as much emphasis as possible on what we are doing with our minds.

In London, when the Dalai Lama first visited and spoke at the magnificent Westminster Cathedral, an architectural wonder begun in the thirteenth century, he said in Tibetan, "I do not care much about buildings." I was stunned, wondering whether this was a diplomatic way to begin a speech. In trepidation, I translated what he said; then he added, "I am interested in what you are doing with your minds." I could not detect any reaction in the audience, but I imagined that, like me, they would quickly come to value his frankness, lack of formality, and constant appeal to the heart.

On another occasion, he was visiting a well-endowed Buddhist monastery in America. Those of us in his party were envious even of the solid oak doors to the rooms. When someone commented on how wonderful the monastery was, he quietly said, "Do they know how to educate?"

Meditation:
Disrupting the Cycle of Ill Deeds
through Equanimity and Contrition

Awareness of death causes us to put less emphasis on externals and more on the internal. Realizing that our actions mold our future, we naturally seek to ameliorate the effects of previous negative karmas. Eventually, a Buddhist seeks to get beyond the cycle of being driven by this uncontrolled process of good and bad karma, to get beyond its influence entirely, while still bringing about others' well-being. But in the meantime, it's necessary to accumulate beneficial karma in order to oppose negative habits and make use of the power of other such positive forces already established in the mind.

How do we break this cycle? Equanimity and contrition are important tools. They are karmically powerful because, with the deliberate practice of equanimity and regret for selfish harm that one has wrought on others, one is not just succumbing to the unhealthy tendency of making oneself the most important or the only one for whom feeling really is important, and turning others into mere objects used for the bringing about of one's own happiness or reducing one's suffering. Instead, one is breaking this cycle—seeing others as equal *beings of feeling* who want happiness and don't want suffering. This is radically different not in the sense of superimposing something from the outside, but of taking common observation of one's own aspirations and applying it to others—and attempting to live within that realization.

Through mental reorientation it is possible to alter the effects of karma. The only sure way of having the presence of mind to affect the course of events is to begin practice before the onset of negative karmic effects, building the strength of familiarity. Once unpleasant karmic results unfold, it's difficult to change one's course *at that time* if you aren't already used to the process. In the midst of an episode it is very difficult to suddenly come to your senses and calm yourself down. But if beforehand you have meditated over and over on how others want happiness and do not want suffering, then your mind will slowly become empowered to notice when anger is beginning to arise and mitigate its force. At the least, if it does arise, its duration will be shorter and the sense of regret stronger.

If you can gradually increase the experience of closeness with others through this type of meditative exercise of equanimity, you can eventually bring that to bear in difficult situations. You develop a reservoir to draw from. You become accustomed to possible ways of relating to people in problem situations other than habitual ways, which are centered around "me first" and aren't very effective.

Sincere contrition is a way of ending guilt and undermining subjugation to the karma of harmful actions both in terms of suffering corresponding effects and of repeating what you have done. Contrition, or regret, is the second of a four-step process—disclosure of ill deeds, contrition, intention of restraint in the future, and virtuous activity—for overcoming the ill-effects of past negative actions.

1. Disclosure of Ill Deeds

In meditation, contemplate: "I have done it; I have to face the fact that I have done it. I can't undo what I did. But I am sorry I did it, and I intend not to do it in the future." Disclosure is the first step in *undoing* guilt, not carrying it all the time but facing misdeeds—"I did it"—not trying to hide them. Hiding what you have done nourishes guilt and thereby increases the negative force of the action—it's as if you are doing the action over and over again.

For contrition to be effective in ameliorating the effects of bad karma, disclosure of those deeds is necessary first. More than simply admitting to misdeeds, disclosure means to uncover, to reveal what you have done. Instead of hiding an action, reveal it. The Dalai Lama said that this is like the splitting of a log: you can see what is inside. Disclosure and contrition cut up, or break up, a mass of nonvirtuous power and diminish its force.

Disclosure acts as an antidote to hatred. By hiding a non-virtuous action, by holding yourself back from others, you separate yourself from those who might learn of your actual deeds. You will hate people who might know what you have done and can identify you. Some of the deeds to be disclosed were probably motivated by hatred, and the past hatred, if not admitted, will lead to future hatred. If you do not reveal misdeeds of body, speech, and mind—if you seek to hide them—their force will increase day by day. Think about it: Someone who feels guilty and tries to hide what he or she has done is nourishing the force of those very deeds.

Physical, verbal, and mental nonvirtuous actions need to be disclosed. You could reveal them to a spiritual guide, but generally people visualize a Buddha or high being in front of them, and reveal to that being what they have done. Go back through your entire life and reveal nonvirtues one by one. It takes time. Or, you could disclose to a group of practitioners. Stop letting those deeds have power over you.

2. Contrition

In meditation, contemplate: "I am sorry I did such and such; I regret it." Contrition is a heartfelt experience of regret that is at the core of resolving guilt. Contrition in itself is not necessarily virtuous; it can even be nonvirtuous. It is possible to regret virtuous actions as well as nonvirtuous ones, so what you decide is right makes a difference. If you give to the poor, for instance, and later regret it, that contrition is a nonvirtue, because the original action of charity was virtuous. What are nonvirtues? They are actions that bring pain—to oneself or others, now or in the future (see pp.169-70). It is possible to bring pain in the future through something that seems pleasurable now.

Sometimes, when I tell friends about some of the wilder activities of my youth, a smirking grin comes over my face as those unkind acts are reviewed. This shows the lack of depth of my contrition, of feeling sorry. Through watching my own reactions, I have found that it is not easy to develop deep contrition, to be truly sorry for misery that I have deliberately caused, to develop regret to the point of feeling that under the same circumstances I would not do the same again. As the years go by, it has been interesting to note how my contrition has deepened.

As I related earlier, as a teenager I was in a juvenile-delinquent gang, and one of the things we would do was frighten people. Any way you could frighten or unsettle people, we would do it—remove the knobs from radios in open cars, scratch cars, pour sugar in gas tanks, run our cars over shrubbery, terrorize hitchhikers, terrorize the people who picked us up hitchhiking, get into fights, remove stop signs, walk into people's houses uninvited, on and on. An old lady would be walking along the street and we would drive right next to her or right up behind her and reach out and slap the side of the car with a thud. She would be frightened, thinking she was going to be run over, and we would all laugh.

Thinking back on it, why did we want to frighten people? Maybe our minds were twisted partly by not wanting to be bound by the rules of the seemingly gutless community we grew up in. Over the years, my regret has grown as I reflect on "Just as I want happiness, don't want suffering, so these others want happiness, don't want suffering." Just as my friend and I worry about each other, hope that we succeed in our various paths, and so forth, so, in a former lifetime, that old lady—defenseless, alone, wanting happiness, not wanting sorrow, out on the road, no one to help her—was my best of friends, and here in this lifetime we have ended up in this perverted relationship. Isn't it sad!

Certain deeds are like coming to a fork in the road. After the deed is done, you remain someone who went down one fork rather than the other; the deed retains power over you. If the deed is nonvirtuous, disclosure and contrition are ways of reducing that power. We cannot undo the past; it is over and done with; but it is possible either to reinforce or to alleviate the force of past actions. That's why disclosure and contrition are powerful.

3. Intention of Restraint in the Future

If guilt means extending worry about what you have done, then it does not help. Buddhism stresses not guilt but contrition followed by developing an intention of restraint in the future. Simply put, you decide that you have done something wrong and then promise not to do it again. Sometimes, some tangible restitution is possible; for example, you can pay damages or return stolen property. But often, the action is over and done with. For instance, if you buy something that does not work, you can return it to the store. But, if you misuse time itself, no matter how much you may regret doing so, you cannot return it. All that is left is an intelligent decision to face what has been done and make a commitment to break the cycle. **In meditation, contemplate: "This action was motivated by desire (or hatred) and ignorance; it was wrong, and I do not want to do it again in the future. May I not do it again in the future! I will make sure not to do it again in the future."**

It is a great relief to feel: "Ten years ago I quarreled with so-and-so. It seemed to be the only thing I could do at the time, but with what I know now, I would not do the same today. I will try never to do that again!"

4. Virtuous Activity

A final way to reinforce disclosure, contrition, and the intention not to repeat the action is to engage in a virtuous activity, such as giving to a charity, giving to beggars, reading profound texts, and so forth, with a deliberate sense that this activity serves as an antidote to what was done earlier.

Death is definite. The time of death is indefinite, uncertain: you could die at any time. So make use of this precious opportunity to do what's worthwhile in the long run. Do the meditations described in this chapter if only for five or ten minutes a day: disclosure of nonvirtues, contrition for having done them, and intention not to repeat them as well as doing a virtuous activity to undermine their force. We need to be reminded of such things because we're habituated in a different direction. If we were really as sensible as we pretend to be, then we'd just have to hear something sensible and it would all fall into place. But it ain't that easy. Meditation is needed.

5

FACING HORROR

_____

S INCE COMPASSION is the wish that beings be free from pain and the causes of pain, it is important to recognize how much our own life and others' lives revolve around feelings. Pleasure, pain, and neutral feelings are emphasized in Buddhist presentations because feelings are so crucial to how we react to persons and events. To generate deep compassion it is necessary to remove barriers to recognizing how strongly our minds are buffeted by feelings.

There are descriptions in Buddhist texts of hells that are temporarily created by a person's own former actions. There is one I particularly dislike in which you are laid out on a table with many other people and someone comes along and draws lines across you. He/she draws many black lines—eight, sixteen, thirty-two—and then takes a saw made of burning iron and cuts your body along the lines. What is the purpose of this description? Is it to cause us to wince? (I am wincing, as I am sure you are.) It is, first of all, to draw out the predispositions to fear that we already have and, second, to give a sense of possible situations of pain. It might seem as though Buddhist teachers are saying, "You have to join our group and pay an entrance fee, because otherwise you will go to hell." But they are not saying this at all; they are pointing out a condition within cyclic existence, also a condition within the mind. I don't know whether anyone in our world has ever been dismembered with a hot saw, but there are people who have been stabbed and hacked to death. It takes work to imagine ourselves in such a situation or to take others undergoing or perpetrating this as objects of compassion, because we tend not to want to see extreme pain and are polarized into distancing ourselves from it.

If it is such a shock to imagine persons being cut by a saw, you can see how quickly we lose the mindset of equanimity or compassion. It is frightening: "Let me out of here! I don't want to see this!" Or it makes us angry: "What is this? What's going on here?" Therefore, the best practitioners are those who, with great enthusiasm, put their mind into every possible situation that they can think of. They read descriptions of the hells and the difficulties of the hungry ghosts; they imagine people attacking them, and they imagine themselves lying there— someone is drawing a line across them, getting the saw ready— and they generate the sense of fright they would have. Within that, they begin to transform their own feeling into compassion for the person who is attacking them. That removes a threshold of hatred. In order to do this, a practitioner has to have great enthusiasm for meditating on individual situations.

We want pleasure and do not want pain, but often we rush

toward pain and away from pleasure. One horrible event has just ended and we're seeking a similar situation all over again. My favorite description of this is of a hell described in Buddhist texts. When you get out of one of the worst hells created by your own karma, you are, of course, tremendously relieved. You come to a hill. On top of the hill is a friend who says, "What are you doing down there? Come on up!" So you start going up, but the hill is made of sharp steel much like a grater. Your flesh is grated on the hillside. Then, when you get to the top, your friend turns into a monster whose mouth opens up and bites your head and you swoon in pain. Doesn't this sound like many relationships?

But the story does not end there. You revive and look down the hill, and now your friend is down there. "What are you doing up on top of the hill? Come on down!" So, you go down the hill and again your flesh is grated. It's called the Iron Grater Hell. You have one pleasurable relationship, it ends up painfully horrible; you seek another pleasurable relationship, and it becomes insufferably horrible; you seek even another relationship. . . I think this is a pattern that most of us play out at one time or another.

Meditation:
Reflecting on Horrible Situations to Increase
Compassion and Equanimity

Horrific descriptions are used to generate a concern for the consequences of actions. They also have another function related to increasing compassion. **In meditation, imagine a** person trapped on the Iron Grater and then from your heart spread out rays of light to enter into this person. The rays of many colors also enter into the Iron Grater, making it a nice, smooth area. The rays of light enter into the two friends, who then act intelligently. It's a powerful technique.

Also, in meditation, imagine somebody crawling on the Iron Grater and contemplate: "Just as I want happiness and don't want suffering, so that person wants happiness and doesn't want suffering." This can be very moving. The image disturbs our persona of calm meditator and brings us into the type of personal confrontation that we experience in daily life. Otherwise, you as the meditator seem rather neutral; it's important to stimulate the mind on many different emotional levels and extend the force of the practice through those levels—imagination is the key.

Begin this practice imagining stronger and then lesser friends, then work with neutral people, and finally work with enemies. Start off picturing in meditation someone as he or she usually is; then imagine that person on the Iron Grater and contemplate: "Just as I want happiness and don't want suffering, Lou wants happiness and doesn't want suffering." Think it to the point where you *feel* it; then pass on to the next person.

Eventually, you will get to enemies. "Enemy" means somebody who has harmed, is harming, or will harm you or your friends. To find enemies, some meditators have to go back to childhood, when the line of friend and enemy was very clear. Sometimes you have to think of a difficult situation. In the middle of that difficult situation, do you have an enemy? For the period of that difficult situation—whether it is thirty seconds, or five minutes, or ten minutes—at that time, do you have an enemy? The more neutral or even kind mind that performs the meditation wouldn't consider this person an enemy, and thus it is necessary to put yourself *within* that agitated situation.

Sometimes a person to whom we are deeply attached does a little thing wrong, and that person immediately is an awful enemy. Suddenly a seemingly serious flaw, unconsciously known but hidden, is seen with overemphasized clarity. Thus even friends, during those periods, are enemies. Attitudes can flip-flop back and forth. This practice is about relationships as we view them not from a distance but right in their center, at the moment.

Practitioners have different reactions to the exercise. You may feel unusual physical sensations when you consider those for whom you have animosity—those you're frustrated with at work, for example. Resistance shows the practice is hitting home. Or, you might feel pity when imagining your enemies because of the ways they've chosen to bring about happiness. What about the last incident with one of your enemies? Could you imagine yourself thinking during that time, "Just as I want happiness, don't want suffering, so this person wants happiness, doesn't want suffering"? When you can do this, the situation will defuse to some extent of its own accord.

Meditation:
Reframing Stressful Situations

Our emotions are built on exaggerating the actual degree of others' goodness or badness. To overcome this, think of problem situations when you flew off the handle, got angry, or where you suffered in silence—each of us has different ways of reacting—and reflect that the person with whom you have difficulties also wants happiness and doesn't want suffering. This type of reflection can open up all sorts of other possibilities as ways of reacting to problem situations.

As a kid, my older brother was (and still is) a good deal bigger than me. I used to wash the dishes and put them in the next sink, and he had to rinse them either with the faucet or with the sprayer attached to a hose. It was one of those old-fashioned sinks, and you had to turn a knob to make the water come out through the sprayer, which was on my side. Sometimes he would want to use the faucet instead of the sprayer, but the water would still be set for the sprayer and this scalding hot water would be let loose onto my side, all this scalding hot water going all over my hands. This happened over and over. It was a situation of great frustration for me. I would scream at him.

One way that I have used to reframe this pivotal memory is to imagine the scene in front of me but as separate from me and reflect that the two boys standing at the sink equally want happiness and don't want suffering. When, after doing that for a while and I have some success, I take it a step further and imagine that I am that child but with a different attitude such that as the hot water is hitting I think, "Just as I want happiness and don't want suffering, so he wants happiness and doesn't want suffering." With practice, this reaches the level of feeling, presenting a horizon of possibilities for different reactions.

Of course, my reaction is not going to be "Come on, Bruce, scald my hand some more" just because I'm recognizing that he wants happiness and doesn't want suffering. But I'm not going to carry on like a maniac every time he does it. I'll figure out a clever technique to get him to remember whether or not he's turned off that knob each time he wants to change from the sprayer to the faucet.

In meditation, search your childhood for such memories and reenter the scene. Then imagine yourself having the presence of mind to think, "Just as I want happiness and don't want suffering, so Priscilla (or whoever) wants happiness and doesn't want suffering."

Think of a few more recent problem situations. Maybe you feel, "Ten years have passed, but I'd do the same thing today as I did then. It was such a difficult situation I'd still fly off the handle today." That would mean that you haven't learned anything in ten years. The practice of equanimity is one way to learn a new perspective and to cause those earlier difficult situations to cease having such a huge influence. Try this new tack; it might not succeed right away, but at least the *possibility* of doing something different enters into the scenario. At that point, the situation's hold on you diminishes.

Meditation:
Extending Equanimity to Nightmare Monsters

The practice of equanimity is particularly helpful for nightmares. Of all the practices you could apply, it is most helpful and comforting, after you have awakened, to generate a sense of equanimity—the similarity of aim—between yourself and the dream-monster. **In meditation, contemplate: "Just as I want happiness and don't want suffering, so that monster wants happiness and doesn't want suffering."**

It might seem weird to reify your own dream objects into sentient beings, since they really do not exist except as figments of the imagination, but try to see the being as wanting happiness and not wanting suffering, as having been a friend, and, when a friend, having extended great kindness. Don't turn this into a test of the meditation. Don't think, "It's got to work on this, and if it doesn't, then the system doesn't work." Just try it, play with it a little. Experience is needed before these meditations will work across boundaries of feeling. But when they do work, you will feel the fear dissipate. We are seeking to disempower a complex that appears as a dream-monster, and the power of equanimity dissolves the fear that empowers the monster. Even when you don't believe it, this technique works. **In meditation, contemplate: "This nightmare-spider, like me, wants happiness and does not want suffering; so may this nightmare-spider have happiness and be free from suffering."**

Let's consider nightmarish figures such as Hitler and Stalin who have appeared in the world. They had very strange ideas about achieving happiness, through bringing extreme pain on others. Nevertheless, no matter how crazy they were, how stupid, how silly, how demented, still—just like me— they wanted happiness and didn't want suffering. I will never decide that their techniques are good, but still, when they had a pain in their back, they wanted relief. They had weird ideas about how to gain happiness and a blindness to recognizing the evidence staring them in the face. But they were still sentient beings.

It helps to think that such powerfully bad persons—or ourselves when we get angry and do nasty things—have fallen out of recognition that other people want happiness and don't want suffering. From this understanding there arises a closeness with those under the influence of strong afflictive emotions.

If you familiarize yourself for a considerable period with these meditations that utilize horrific situations for increasing equanimity, reflecting on many individual people, gradually your sense of equanimity, an even-mindedness, will extend to anyone who appears.

LIFETIMES

Meditation: The Rebirth Game

OVER THE COURSE of our lifetimes, each person we know or meet has equally been a friend, an enemy, and a neutral person. Whether or not you believe in reincarnation, let's play the game of rebirth. If you have a hunch that rebirth does indeed occur, the exercise may be easier, but even if you don't, we can still play the game. Just as when we watch a movie and get involved and develop all sorts of attitudes, so here we are creating certain feelings for the sake of seeing what happens in our own minds. **In meditation, contemplate: "Five lifetimes ago, I was born in Egypt (or any country of your choosing) where I was a small shopkeeper. I had several friends and several enemies, and the rest were, to me, neutral."** Imagine the scene; feel your presence there.

If rebirth is true, would it be the case that the best of your friends in the present lifetime was the best of your friends five lifetimes ago? Possibly, but not necessarily. Could it be that the best of your friends was neutral—somebody whom you saw on the street and ignored with an attitude of indifference, or even neglect? You just didn't care. In this lifetime, when you are sick, your friend is deeply concerned, and when your friend is ill, you are deeply concerned. Could it be the case that six lifetimes ago this person was your enemy?

Friends and enemies switch back and forth even in this lifetime. Do you have a friend who was an enemy earlier in this lifetime? We can also get super angry and direct enemy-type energy at loved ones. Therefore, this other person whom today you reject or feel indifferent about was actually—in former lifetimes—as close to you as your good friends, or was as distant from you as your worst enemy. Wouldn't that be the case if there is rebirth, if there's no single beginning?

Countrywise, the Russians used to be the great enemies. Growing up in the '40s and '50s as I did, they were clearly the worst enemy you could possibly imagine, just unthinkably gross beings; today I see that they are like everyone else. China was a close friend of the U.S. during the Second World War, then became an enemy during the Korean War, and now is supposedly a political friend again, although their extremely harsh treatment of Tibet is often disregarded. In politics, the switch is easy, and the blindness just as great as it is in personal relationships.

An article in *Time* magazine during the Vietnam War made fun of the Vietnamese for taking care of flies as if the flies were their grandmothers. The article made this sound absurd. In a Tibetan monastery you come up from behind a fly and *whoosh!* you grab it cupped in your hand and take it out the door. In

India, Tibetans gently lower a plastic bag over a fly, and when it flies up to the top of the bag, they squeeze the bag in the middle, and then gather up several other flies in the same way, finally going to the door and letting them go. Imagine the care they show for this other living being. Such an attitude about caring for another being is the point that the *Time* article missed.

Over the course of lifetimes, a person who now is the best of your friends could have been a fly, and people you encounter who act gruffly or indifferently to you could have been your best friends. Our attitudes about others have to be changed to take into account this changeability. Even nowadays, some friends are sunny-day friends but not rainy-day friends. So, it is by circumstances that friends, neutral people, and enemies move from this group to that group.

There's no definiteness with regard to any friend—that this person always was friendly in the past. In fact, it's likely that the person was an enemy at some time—even several times— over the course of lifetimes. Once we assume that the course of lifetimes has no beginning, we can surmise that at least several times our good friend must have been a terrible enemy. It's disruptive to think this way, for you begin wondering, "Is this system of meditation aimed at making everyone into enemies, disrupting my friendships?" Indeed, since everyone has been in every possible relationship with us in the past, they've all been our enemies; should we consider them to be enemies?

Also, if everyone has been a neutral person in the past, how are we supposed to feel now? Indifferent to everyone? This system claiming to cultivate compassion itself begins to seem offensive.

However, the process is aimed first at making everyone equal, and then at making everyone close. Still, if it works, it will be disruptive, not easy. If the process doesn't touch you, it will just be words: "Everyone was friend, everyone was neutral person, everyone was enemy. Let's all be friends. It's great. We all love each other." And then we'll fight over a parking place, or whatever.

Let's consider neutral people. You recently saw someone driving along the highway. Maybe whizzing by. This certainly is a neutral person. Or a cashier in the supermarket. Is it likely this person was a friend in a former lifetime? You feel some resistance to thinking this, but of course it's likely that the person was indeed a friend. At minimum, you couldn't say this neutral person definitely wasn't a friend. Also at some time in the past, he or she was an enemy who would have liked to see you fail.

Enemies could easily have been friends in the past, too, as well as neutral people. You can see how your sense of time is being expanded. Not only are you extending your mind, extending your relationships, to many, many sentient beings throughout space; you are also expanding your sense of time. There is no place where you have not been born in the past; there is no era in which you did not live; you cannot point to any place and say, "I was never born there."

When cultivating equanimity through this technique, it can be helpful to start with neutral people, because it is easier to

come alive to the possibility that someone for whom you pres-
ently have no particular emotional investment one way or the
other was in the past a friend and, at other times, an enemy. If
you're good at visualizing, imagine the person in front of you
and perhaps in her own environment. If you're not good at
visualizing, feel the presence of the person. **In meditation, contemplate: "This person was my friend"—you can be specific
about it—"two lifetimes ago. We were so close," and make it
come home to you by analogy, "just like my best friend and I
are now."** Feel really close to this person, concerned over each
other, wanting to know each other's thoughts, reactions.

The steps in the cultivation of compassion are said to be easy
to explain but hard to do. And you can see why; the mind is
like a large number of many magnets—conflicting emotions—
with certain forces that pull on each other, and the process
of this meditation disturbs the present arrangement of those
forces. There are many other obstacles, too. For instance, some
practitioners find that the so-called neutral person, once imagined, becomes either friend or enemy. Maybe he or she is good-
looking, so you start getting desirously involved. He or she
is no longer neutral. You lose the sense of what it means for
someone to be neutral. How do you proceed? This is one way
the meditation of equanimity (and thus the subsequent steps
for generating compassion to be explained in later chapters)
is difficult.

As an antidote to this blockage, consider this: As soon as
you take this person to mind, she's either helpful or harmful
because you're either attracted or not attracted to her, but the

degree of attraction or dislike is different from usual attraction and repulsion. She still isn't someone who manifestly helped or harmed you; you haven't been overtly involved with her. Notice how like and dislike interfere, based on mere possibilities that can occur when visualizing or feeling the presence of a neutral person. Notice how these interests rule our attitudes.

Don't make a test for neutrality that's so difficult that no one could pass it. For me, some of the best neutral people are those with whom I've had contact and can recognize, such as a storekeeper or a checkout person. If you have difficulty with that, try people who are just passing by in the street. But it is also helpful to include people whom you recognize, such as the person who regularly cleans your office.

You might wonder how someone who was close in a previous life could now be distant, but it's really no different than going to a class reunion and failing to recognize an old close friend or a strong enemy. This happened to me nine years ago. A fellow stopped me—I was wearing a name tag—and asked, "Are you Jeff Hopkins?" "Yes." "Well, then I guess you're him." He couldn't believe it was me, but, even worse, when he told me his name, I couldn't remember him. In time I remembered that he was the friend with whom I shared my deepest thoughts and hopes in the fourth grade.

The first time I went to India I shaved off my beard after a few months, and people got used to me without it. The second time I went, I had a beard. A friend came to Dharamsala from Nepal. I saw him from my window and called out to him. He looked up at me but kept walking. I came out of the house and called him again, and he looked up and said, "Oh yes, hello." I told him my name, and he was happy to see me, but he asked, "What happened to you? Did someone die? Has there been an accident?" He could have passed by me without knowing who I was and without a second thought, but after he recognized me, he was tremendously concerned because I looked so different; then he affectionately remembered me as the friend who taught him Tibetan grammar.

Once the implications of multiple lifetimes hit home, you may even feel sad—that we were that closely bonded and yet we have no memory of it now. Stay with the meditation—feel it. This contemplation is easier toward a neutral person because we're stuck on neither the attachment side nor the hatred side. But if you succeed, it's still shocking.

After absorbing those implications without rushing, reflect that this neutral person, who is neither helping nor harming you in this lifetime, was an enemy in the last lifetime just as so-and-so is now—someone who was delighted when I failed and really wanted to do me in.

Don't create a definition for "enemy" that's so difficult that you deceive yourself into thinking, "Oh, I don't have any enemies." We all have enemies, even if only for a moment. For example, there's that son of a bitch who's taking the biggest piece of cake today just like yesterday. You might resist thinking of him as an enemy: "But I'm not so superficial as to dislike a person because of taking the biggest piece of cake." But you are nevertheless frustrated. Those people who are the objects of your frustration, even though in general you might not class them as enemies, are enemies for *that* mind at *that* time. Watch *that* mind; stay with it.

At a meditation seminar, a retreatant told me he was having trouble finding neutral people, so he imagined going to the movies. He was able to consider the people sitting next to him in the imagined theater and transform his relationship to them, but then at one point they all turned on him—there were two hundred people not very happy about his meditating on them! He had to face the obstacle and keep working.

So, don't think this exercise will be easy. As I said earlier, it's easy to outline this series of meditations that begins with the foundational cultivation of equanimity and proceeds through several other meditations (yet to be described) that result in profound altruism—but it's hard to do, because our minds are structured in hidden, counterproductive patterns. The retreatant's hidden paranoia rose to the surface, and he was immediately faced with having to deal with enemies.

If you can recall childhood attitudes, go through your childhood classes and think about the neutral people, the enemies, and so forth. They're *really* enemies. When I went to kindergarten and first grade, I was amazed. Everybody was saying "kill": "My mother's going to kill me." "If I don't eat my lunch, my mother will kill me." "I want to kill so-and-so." I was stunned—what were they talking about?

You may think you couldn't forgive savage cruelty—Stalin, for instance. But have you ever been cruel to anyone, in even a small way? My oldest brother worked on a farm where they were raising pheasants for people to kill. One day I went into the pheasant house, cornered a pheasant, and threw stones at it, to kill it. But I've done worse things. I've done really nasty things to people, got some idea in my head, and carried it out. Stalin too got some real nasty ideas in his mind, and got into a position where he could carry them out on a broad scale.

Killing millions of people is indeed on a different scale from what most of us have done in this lifetime; however, just as when you work on a small scale you spend twenty-four hours on that scale, so when you work on a big scale you still have the same twenty-four hours, but you've got all sorts of people under you. You say, "Go to such-and-such region and kill a hundred thousand people," rather than just telling someone to go to hell. By reflecting this way, you can begin to get glimpses of how even hated persons are similar to yourself in wanting happiness and not wanting suffering but often engage in counterproductive techniques to accomplish these. Your mind will loosen, relax, and free itself from singlepointed hatred.

COUNTERPRODUCTIVE ADDICTIONS: EIGHT CONFINING CONCERNS

The reason why we are so vulnerable to afflictive emotions like hatred is that our minds usually fall into the habitual patterns of what Buddhists call the eight confining concerns—like and dislike, gaining and losing, praise and blame, fame and disgrace—which are defined as follows:

1. Like: Being overly attached to this person or situation, finding it impossible to live without him, her, or it. For example, I lust after coffee frozen yogurt and don't much

like chocolate-cherry. It almost seems that if I were not concerned about these, I wouldn't have anything left to do!

2. Dislike: Being utterly unable to stand certain persons or situations—feeling you just *have* to get the person out of your sight.

3. Gaining: Being fixated about getting a certain advantage. For example, a promotion or raise becomes so important that it almost becomes the rationale for existing.

4. Losing: Worrying endlessly about advantages slipping away. Will it really help to worry about health, wealth, and friends most of the day?

5. Praise: Scurrying after others' approbation. Like a child given a piece of candy, when we are praised, it is as if we have been given the world. This is silly.

6. Blame: Uselessly trying to escape from blame. We can even get sick worrying that someone might stick a finger in our face. At other times, we get defensive to ward off the words; and at still other times, we take the offensive— "The best defense is a good offense."

7. Fame: Thirsting after widespread renown. Today as I write this, an article about me is coming out in a big-city newspaper. Am I excited!

8. Disgrace: Fearing bad words, even if true, might spread around. The same article, if it misreports something I said or maybe offends the very people I am trying to help, will bring me disrepute; so I alternate between glee and apprehension—how useless!

Once we're in the grip of any of the eight confining concerns, it is difficult to remember that everyone wants happiness and doesn't want suffering. Caught in such self-centered matters, we can't consider that those who prevent us from getting our likes and give us our dislikes want happiness and don't want suffering. Or that these people who are providing us with blame and disgrace and not fame and praise all want happiness and don't want suffering, just as we do. Once we're sunk in these selfish activities, the sense of commonality among beings is lost.

However, when you loosen the eight confining concerns a little, more room is left to recognize that not just you but all people want pleasure and don't want pain. Then, the more equanimity you have, fixation on these counterproductive pursuits decreases. This person who's preventing me from gaining my cone of coffee frozen yogurt by taking the last dip wants happiness and doesn't want suffering—by reflecting on that, my fixation on getting it does indeed diminish.

Do you think you'd lose out if you recognized that everyone, like yourself, equally wants happiness and doesn't want suffering? What would be the reasons not to engage in such thought? The eight confining concerns. "If I don't disregard others, how can I make a big push for myself at my job? I'd lose the chance to jump forward right at the time when something good was about to happen, and thus I'd lose out." Would you? Maybe, if you let go of your attachment to gaining, praise, and fame, you would gain what you're usually seeking—other people's friendship, esteem, some kindness. You get angry when other people aren't kind to you! Yet if you had this more compassionate attitude, you'd have the esteem of others, and people would be expressing kindness.

Would you be weak? Don't we sometimes think of the compassionate as nice but basically stupid? And the smart as hateful? The smart as analytical, ruthless, scheming? I don't think it has to be this way. It takes such great strength of mind to maintain the attitude of equanimity that there'd be no chance you could be weak—as long as you weren't just maintaining it with a few people. If you can maintain it with enemies, of course you have to have a strong mind.

It is critical in some jobs to thrust yourself forward, to get your ideas across and advance. But that does not mean that you need to disregard others' feelings in order to push for your way. Rather, if you keep in mind that people want happiness and don't want suffering, you understand their basic orientation. Your judgment is not clouded by a fundamental ignorance, and so you notice opportunities even for sticking your nose forward all the better. You couldn't do something that was to the detriment of other people *and* maintain knowledge that other people want happiness and don't want suffering, just like yourself. Establish this closeness. It would be very difficult to cheat, to step forward and cheat other people.

Do you think you'd have to trust everyone? *No!* Ridiculous. In fact, you'd probably be all the more clever at being suspicious of others' motives when necessary. Once you know they want happiness and don't want suffering, you know they'll do most anything they can to get it!

Still, if there's one piece of cake left, give it away. And that's hard, very hard.

One implication of rebirth, of having been associated with others in many situations, is that we should take joy in their success, thereby undermining the hold of worldly concerns. Take a simple example: Suppose you've looked hard for a parking place and finally see it, but somebody comes and takes it. Why get involved in confining thoughts of getting and losing? It's rather useless to feel, "Hey, you son of a bitch, you took my space!" That person's quite happy: "I got a space!" Why not take delight in that other person's finding a place? Complaining won't help anyway. You were not even giving up the parking place; you saw it, and as you were driving your car there, someone beat you to it. Why not take delight in that person's joy at getting a parking place? Why not? Nothing to lose. You're frustrated at the person because your pleasure at finding a parking place was blocked, but you make yourself even more unhappy by carrying on about it, which in the long run is indeed insignificant. Try it; see how it feels.

In time, the practice of equanimity, which initially may appear as if it would put us in a position of weakness and loss, is quite the opposite. It puts us in a position of strength and of gain. At that point, you understand that the failure to maintain recognition that others want happiness, don't want suffering is what brings about real loss, and truly makes you lose out.

Although the practice of equanimity yields a sense of similarity and thus closeness to everyone, something basically pleasant in everyone, it doesn't mean that you look for some feature other than this basic aspiration to happiness. For instance, what are you going to do with a mass murderer? Are you going to say, "He speaks well"? And if so, does that override all his faults? "Oh, his faults. He killed many, many people, but he speaks well. And he's jovial over dinner, so I like him." Impossible! You don't have to look for something like that. The mere fact that he's a sentient being, wants happiness and doesn't want suffering, *that's* sufficient. Isn't it? The point is that you don't need to make up other things or just emphasize the person's good qualities, blotting out the other qualities.

It's difficult. I used to live on Fourteenth Street in Charlottesville at the bottom of a hill, and cars always whizzed by. I got fed up with it. I'd be trying to meditate and hear *whoosh whoosh whoosh*. After a while I'd think, "Why the hell do they always want to go this way and that way?" But then when I thought, "There goes another sentient being. Wow! There goes another sentient being," it's rather pleasant.

So, in sum, if you come upon blocks preventing recognition that a particular person is like yourself in the basic aspiration to happiness, you might reflect on the eight confining concerns and imagine what life would be like if you didn't care *so* much about like, dislike, gaining, losing, praise, blame, fame, and disgrace.

SUMMING UP THE PRACTICE OF EQUANIMITY

We are aiming to develop a strong feeling of love and compassion with respect to everyone, but this cannot be done without first seeing an equality of all beings through meditatively cultivating equanimity. Otherwise, you'll easily be able to generate love and compassion for friends and may be able to extend a little of this to neutral people, but even minor enemies will remain a huge problem. Thus at first it is necessary to recognize how friends, neutral persons, and enemies are equal.

This is done in two ways. One way to break down rigid classifications of people is by reflecting first with respect to friends, then neutral persons, and then enemies:

> Just as I want happiness and don't want suffering, so this friend wants happiness and doesn't want suffering. And equally, this neutral person wants happiness and doesn't want suffering. And equally, this enemy wants happiness and doesn't want suffering.

Another way is to reflect on what your relationships have been with others over the course of lifetimes, beginning with neutral persons, then friends, and finally enemies. An enemy in this lifetime wants to do you in, but over the course of lifetimes was this person just an enemy? No. If you do not believe in rebirth, utilize the rebirth game, the rebirth perspective, as a technique for making your mind more flexible.

Either of these techniques will work:

+ Reflecting on the similarity of yourself and others in the basic aspiration to gain happiness and be rid of suffering
+ Reflecting on the changeability of relationships over the course of lifetimes

Gradually these practices will make it such that nobody is one-pointedly in any of these categories, and if you can alternate back and forth between both techniques, they fortify each other. The rigidity of the categories of beings is broken down in order to make a smoother field so that the crop of compassion can be planted. The process is also likened to smoothing a wall so that the mural of compassion can be painted. Otherwise, you will continue to adhere to certain people as just enemies. Unless you eventually recognize and confront problems with particular persons that you have marked off as indelibly nasty, they will become an obstacle later to universal compassion—they will be outside of the sphere. Bring them into this sphere by reflecting on how, just as much as your good friend wants happiness and doesn't want suffering, they want happiness and don't want suffering. It has tremendous impact.

Which is stronger for you in developing equanimity? The first meditation:

> Just as I want happiness and don't want suffering, so
> Betty wants happiness and doesn't want suffering.

Or the second meditation:

> Over the course of lifetimes Betty has been friend,
> neutral person, and enemy numerous times.

For me, both are effective but with different impacts.

Go through everyone you've ever known, contemplating in these ways. After I had practiced this over several months, my first teacher, the Kalmyk Mongolian scholar-adept Geshe Wangyal, had me stay up all night doing this.

As discussed previously, at the end of a session of meditation, remember to dedicate its value to the welfare of many different sentient beings. This is a way for us to get out of paranoia, and for us to face our hated enemies. It is most powerful to dedicate the value of one's own virtue to such strong, ignorant people. May they gain some advancement from it.

Now that you have practiced equanimity, along with several booster meditations, you have a firm foundation for the remaining meditations leading to compassion. These are explained in the following chapters.

STEP TWO

RECOGNIZING FRIENDS

EVERYONE AS A FRIEND

Meditation:

Cultivating Closeness, an Appeal to Common Experience

HOW SHOULD we view sentient beings? If they have all been in every possible relationship with us from time without beginning (and time has no beginning in Buddhism), should we consider them to be enemies? Everyone has indeed been the enemy—the person who wants me to trip, fall down the stairs, break a leg. Geshe Wangyal said that one problem with this outlook would be that you'd have to go out and kill everybody. Difficult to do. Everyone has also been neutral, like the many people we pass on the streets; we may even know some faces, but we don't have any open relationship with them. They are just people working here or there; we may see them often, but there is neither desire nor hatred. Should we consider them to be neutral? Or should we consider these people to be friends?

The answer given by popular early-twentieth-century Tibetan lama Pa-bong-ka is provocative. It is not an abstract principle, but refers to common experience. To render it in my own words: If your close friend became crazed and attacked you with a knife, you would attempt to relieve him of the knife and get his mind back in its natural state; you would use the appropriate means to take the knife, but you wouldn't then kick him in the head.

Pa-bong-ka himself uses the example of one's own mother: If your mother became crazed and attacked you with a knife, you would relieve her of the knife. You would not then proceed to beat her up. That's his appeal: Once there's a profoundly close relationship, the close relationship predominates. Why is a friend acting so terribly? Why is she turning against you and attacking you? It's due to a counterproductive attitude—a distortion—in the person's mind.

Indeed, if your own best friend went mad and came at you with a knife to kill you, what would you do? You would seek to disarm your friend, but then you would not proceed to beat the person, would you? You would disarm the attacker in whatever way you could—you might even have to hit the person in order to disarm him, but once you had managed to disarm him, you would not go on to hurt him. Why? Because he is close to you.

If you felt that everyone in the whole universe was in the same relationship to you as your very best friend and if you saw anyone who attacked you as your best friend gone mad, you would not respond with hatred. You would respond with behavior that was appropriate, but you would not be seeking to retaliate and harm the person out of hatred. He would be too dear to you.

Therefore, in teaching compassion, Buddhists do not choose a neutral person as the example of all sentient beings; they choose the strongest of all examples, their best friend. Your feeling for that person is the feeling you should ideally have for every sentient being. You cannot go up to the police officer on the corner and hug her. But you can, inwardly, value her, as well as all sentient beings, as your best friend.

So if everyone in the past has been close, then there is good reason that closeness should predominate. And this becomes a reason—in addition to the similarity between oneself and others—for meditatively cultivating love and compassion, rather than hatred and distance, with respect to everyone. It is not sufficient merely to see that sentient beings are suffering. You must also develop a sense of closeness with them, a sense that they are dear. With that combination—seeing that people suffer and thinking of them as dear—you can develop compassion. So, after meditatively transforming your attitude toward friends, enemies, and neutral persons such that you have gained progress in becoming even-minded toward all of them, the next step is to meditate on everyone as friends, to *feel* that they have been profoundly close.

In meditation, take individual persons to mind, starting with your friends. Reflect on how close your best friend is— recognize your attitude, for example, when your friend needs your concern, like when she's ill. This is an appeal to common experience—to how we already naturally react to close friends. **Then, in meditation, extend this feeling to more beings.**

First you need to recognize people as having been friend, enemy, and neutral person countless times over countless lifetimes—or at least you can't say that there isn't anyone who hasn't been a friend, or you can't say there isn't anyone who hasn't been an enemy, or you can't say with surety that there's anyone who hasn't been neutral. Once you recognize this, it's possible to begin to recognize everyone as friends.

To consider ourselves dear we usually do not have to enter into meditation. We cherish ourselves greatly. When we see ourselves suffering, we have no problem in wishing to escape that suffering. The problem lies in not cherishing others. The ability to cherish others has to be cultivated. **In meditation:**

1. **Visualize someone you like very much and then super-impose the image of someone toward whom you are neutral. Alternate between the two images until you value the person toward whom you are neutral as much as the friend.**
2. **Then superimpose, in succession, the images of a number of people toward whom you are neutral, until you value each of them as much as the greatest of friends.**
3. **When you have developed facility with those two steps, it is possible to extend the meditation to enemies.**

For me, it's much more disruptive to think about my friends as having been enemies than it is to think about my enemies as having been friends. No matter how difficult it is to think of a hated enemy as having been a close friend in a recent lifetime, it's more disruptive to think of my close friend as having been an enemy. With regard to neutral people, it's shocking, a whole new perspective, to think, "Just two lifetimes ago, we were very close friends, and now by the force of our own actions we don't even know each other, don't even care about each other, we neglect each other, we're indifferent."

Is it convincing to base subsequent practices on this notion of cross-positioning over the course of lives? I think it is, but success in changing attitudes certainly isn't easy to achieve since it depends on either a belief in rebirth or a willingness to play out the rebirth perspective. Nevertheless, both of these provide a strong foundation, whereas if the appeal was to an abstract principle or because Buddha said so, it would be all right for a day or two but would not be profoundly moving.

The other approach—that doesn't rely on rebirth—is merely that we're all equal in wanting happiness and not wanting suffering. And if it's worthwhile for me to gain happiness, then it's worthwhile for everyone else to gain happiness. Noticing this similarity makes us close. The late-fourteenth- and early-fifteenth-century yogi-scholar Dzong-ka-ba says that in order to generate compassion, it is necessary to understand how beings suffer *and* to have a sense of closeness to them. He says that otherwise, when you understand how they suffer, you'll take delight in it. For example, so-and-so enemy just got liver disease, and you think, "Good riddance. She's getting what she deserves."

Thus, in order to care for other beings, it's not sufficient merely to know that they suffer, or even how they suffer, because knowledge that a person is suffering this way might make you happy, especially if that person is an enemy. "May this person be run over." We all have such thoughts due to a lack of intimacy. Not only must we know the depths of their suffering, but they must be *dear* to us. In short, for compassion to develop toward a wide range of persons, mere knowledge of how beings suffer is not sufficient; there has to be a sense of closeness with regard to every being. That intimacy is established either through merely reflecting that everyone equally wants happiness and doesn't want suffering, or through reflecting on the implications of rebirth, or both, with the one reinforcing the other. Both techniques rely on noticing our own common experience and extending its implications to others.

THE THREE TYPES OF SUFFERING

Knowledge of how beings suffer has to come through reflecting on the various levels of suffering. It's easy to have compassion for the poor, difficult to have compassion for the rich. We don't understand the depths of suffering. At minimum, the rich have in their continuums all the causes of becoming poor. Over limitless lifetimes, they have engaged in actions that have established predispositions that, when activated, will lead to lifetimes of poverty. So in the long run, we are all similar even from that point of view. Never mind also similar from the point of view of being caught in a process that is beyond our own control.

All too often, our compassion and our ability to recognize suffering vary based on the situation. We have less compassion for the intelligent, the handsome and beautiful, the rich, the healthy, and the happy. Even amongst the poor, you learn that you have easy compassion for those who are both cute and poor, but for those who are poor but not cute, it's rather difficult. And then it's all the more difficult for those impoverished people who have an evil attitude toward you and would just as soon see you dead. Right? Or beggars who are maiming their own children so that they can be more pathetic as beggars. Very difficult to have compassion for them. But of course they are more deserving of compassion in some sense because they've sunk so low.

What, then, are the types of suffering? There are three types.

1. The first is the suffering of misery, which refers to physical and mental pain. This is obvious suffering, but not everyone has it all of the time.
2. The second is the suffering of change. The suffering of change is more difficult to realize as being painful than that of misery. The suffering of change refers to usual happiness—happiness because such pleasure can turn into pain. If something has an ultimate nature of pleasure, no matter how many times or how long one engages in it, it will still generate pleasure, but if it does not have such a nature, it turns into pain. If you want some pizza, for example, and you eat it, there is the joy of getting the pizza in your mouth, but then, if you persist at eating it, after a while you get sick. The suffering of change refers to experiences as simple as that. Ordinary sexual pleasure

is also included because, if you have too much of it, eventually it is no longer pleasurable and can even become painful. This doesn't mean that the feeling of pleasure is the feeling of pain. The feeling of pleasure is pleasurable, but when you look at it from another point of view, it is not pleasurable by way of its own nature because it can turn into pain. Often we think, "How wonderful it would be to have this!" and it quickly turns into a mess. If something is ultimately a source of pleasure, why does it not give pleasure whenever we contact it, and why doesn't the pleasure last? Someone who is sick in the hospital with severe intestinal problems won't be interested at all in an attractive man or woman. And if the things we buy were actually sources of pleasure, as we expect them to be, we would be satisfied with a few of these things in our homes. We wouldn't have to go out week after week and buy new things. That is the suffering of change.

3. The third type of suffering is the suffering of pervasive conditioning. Realization of the suffering of pervasive conditioning is a big step. Our minds and bodies are such that what happens to them is not under our own control. Usually, we live without any thought about the fact that we are not under our own power. We want to be happy, so we do anything we can to get ourselves into situations in which we won't remember that this fact is a condition of life. One of my good friends, the head of the Buddhist Studies program at the University of Wisconsin, went to his cellar to light his gas hot-water heater one night, but

gas had escaped and blew up when he struck the match. He was temporarily staying in a small house with a cellar made of cement blocks. I saw a picture of the cellar later; the explosion moved a whole line of blocks around the cellar about one inch. He was a strong man. He managed to walk upstairs, and he lived for a month and then died. It was hard to account for what had happened; he was so strong. You had to agree with him or fight him—he preferred a fight. You felt that he wouldn't even have to turn pages to read a book; a white light would penetrate it. You felt, "Who could stop him?" That's the suffering of pervasive conditioning—being under the influence of a process not under one's own control.

Thus, when Buddhists think of sentient beings qualified by suffering, they are thinking of (1) physical and mental suffering, (2) that even our happiness can be seen as a type of suffering, and (3) that we are under the control of a process of conditioning. In this way, everyone is undergoing suffering; all have the last type, and most have the other two.

Meditation:
Your Best Friend as the Model for Everyone
Who's your best friend? **Take the person who appears in your mind, and then consider your next best friend. Recognize that friend number two was just like friend number one in a former lifetime. Gradually, person by person, go through and identify that all of your other friends have been like this**

best of friends in former lifetimes, at some time, even several times. Then take neutral people. Then start with the least of enemies, and work on down to the worst of enemies. The practice is staged this way, beginning with friends, then with neutral people, and then with the least of enemies, so that you can build up experience with what it means to recognize someone as having been a best friend in a former lifetime. Otherwise, if I jumped to considering an enemy, I'd have a weak sense of him as a friend, at best; most likely I'd just deceive myself, due to having nothing against which to measure the experience of recognition as a friend, nothing to indicate how long I'll have to meditate, nothing to prod me on to more reflection so that my feeling will become deeper, more moving. I would easily be satisfied with a superficial declaration that five lifetimes ago my present foe was my best of friends, and then get on to the next topic.

However, when you start with your number two friend, recognizing that person to be like number one, you can get an intimate feeling of their sameness as best of friends, reflecting on scenarios such as I could with a friend whom I haven't seen in twenty years. **In meditation, contemplate: "Just as he and I have been separate for twenty years, but we still think about each other with strong fondness, so this other friend, though not now this close, was just as intimate in the last lifetime."** Keep reflecting this way, using details of your relationship with the present best friend to evoke the feeling of such strong association, and extend it to the other person, contemplating in detail until you experience a change of attitude.

When the feeling comes, you'll notice it—it will be so vivid, so refreshing. Remain with this new attitude for a while; don't race on to number three friend. Savor the new knowledge.

To repeat: **In meditation, reflect: "Number two friend was just like old Mike; three lifetimes ago we cared for each other in just the same way."** Feel it. Recognize it.

Could you use your lama or guru as the model for the best of friends? Your guru is in many respects the best of friends, but that's not the sort of friend that's being called for in this exercise. Tibetans use one's mother as the primary example of the best of friends. However, this sometimes doesn't work so well in other cultures, since parental relationships are often difficult. In such cases, if you forced yourself to use your mother, or father, to be the model, you would be, in effect, cultivating all people as enemies. In that case, use your closest friend.

It may seem selfish to use your best friend or best provider as the example of all sentient beings merely because that person helped you. It may also seem superficial to merely reflect on a person's kindness to you. Also, the person's kindness, as a mother or as a friend, is usually dependent on attachment. There's a wrong element to it. Most mothers have tremendous feeling for their own children; if one of her children is challenged, she behaves like a bear, scaring away the other children, but when her own child challenges another child, she is not quite as fierce; she may scold her child, but she has a different feeling for her own child, maybe even praising the child's courage.

Nevertheless, it is the element not of attachment but of

closeness that is being emphasized. The essential idea is that there has been a strong relationship with your own friend or mother. The Tibetan emphasis on the mother as the best of friends is a psychological key based on a relationship early in our lives. As those who have children, or who have observed people with children, know, the child is extremely attached to the mother—the feeling of protection, of unconditional love, the very warmth of it all. For example, the child runs to the mother and grabs her leg and holds on. At some point as we grow up, we usually deny this feeling or push it away or change it, but in order to develop a truly strong feeling for all sentient beings, it is necessary to reawaken it.

I had a very difficult relationship with my mother after around age twelve, and thus I used somebody else as the model. In time, when meditating on the enemy class, I came to her, not the worst of enemies, but down there pretty low. Reflecting on her as having been the best of friends in a former lifetime—meditating on her only after I had experienced what this meant through considering a multitude of friends, neutral persons, and less severe enemies—eventually caused me to evoke what my feelings toward her were like as a small child, and she suddenly jumped over into the best of friends category. Sometimes she'd jump back to the enemy class, too.

So, the Tibetan choice of the mother as this primary example of a close friend is a provocative piece of psychology. After all, the mother is the first "other" in the lifetime, and many of our relationships are structured around that, whether we like it or not. So it's a great key to use the mother, *eventually*. There are very strong positive feelings tied up with one's mother, and thus, if you can't recall and thereby unleash them, there's a lid on your compassion, just because there's a lid on these strong feelings. The attachment to our mothers is that great.

I don't at all recommend forcing yourself to take your mother as the model of the closest friend, but I do suggest being open to the reawakening of childhood feelings. In my own experience, they are so strong that when you do reawaken them—when they do battle with the later difficult feelings—they win rather easily, because they are deep-seated.

It's interesting how we freeze our view of particular people. We exaggerate certain aspects we see in others, thereby freezing them into narrow, unproductive categories of relationships and limiting our ability to feel close and act out of a sense of intimacy. We lock them into certain patterns of behavior, and then, because we see these attitudes as solid, influence others to stay in those patterns: "This person is just. . ." But when you think and feel, "Two lifetimes ago this person was my best friend," the possibilities with that person now in this life open up. Consider a coworker, a colleague, a fellow student; you don't have to think about her in just the limited way that you have been. "She was a great friend in the past. I doubt she's going to be my best friend in this lifetime, but there's no reason to have frozen her into the particular mind-set I found myself in yesterday." All sorts of possibilities open up.

Here in this meditation of recognizing others as having been our best friend, we are loosening that process by superimposing the "best friend" feeling on lesser ones. We're becoming much more flexible. The practice reveals a plenitude of possibilities with others. What would it be like for these people if we acted this way with them, not externally but internally? If, when we saw them, we had an internal feeling of such strong intimacy— if we had an internal feeling of, "Oh, I'm meeting with my best of friends"—how do you think this would affect others? What would happen if we inwardly treated strangers in stores as best of friends? There would be a greater warmth and a considerable amount of extra, flexible energy available both to us and the world.

Recently, I recalled a bothersome incident with my mother. I had come home during my first year at college and was enthusiastically explaining to her about the fascinating courses I was taking in psychology, anthropology, and English and American literature. She bitterly resented the fact that she had not attended college and also had an antipathy to intellectual enthusiasm even though she was intellectually active herself. Much like my grade school experiences when I would come home and tell her what was happening and she would start criticizing me bitterly to the point that I shut up, she launched into her invective. We ended up with her in the kitchen on one side of the house and me on the other in the living room in a bright, light blue rocking chair that she had painted and stenciled. We were literally screaming at each other. I so deeply wanted to get back on the bus and return to college and my studies, but I didn't; I remained in a suffocating scream. I have often thought, "What would have happened in my life had I just walked out and gotten on the bus down the road?" And I thought it again the other day when this scene reappeared in my mind. Then suddenly it occurred to me that I should reflect, within the body of the person screaming from the living room, "Just as I want happiness and don't want suffering, so Mother (that's what we called her) wants happiness and doesn't want suffering." Wow! What a revolution! No need to leave; within that same body, I calmed down with a poignant sense of how she caused so much misery for herself—she'd get so angry on the telephone with her best woman-friend that she would literally hold the phone from her face and scream into it! I cannot put into words my sense of commiseration. Also, the sense that I had found a road out of that scream from the living room without taking the bus back to college. What a relief!

MAKING PROGRESS

PROCEEDING GRADUALLY

IN THE EXERCISE of meditating on all beings as friends, you consider that each person in a former lifetime was just as close as your close friends are now: "In a former lifetime, this person was as dear to me as my best friend in this lifetime." You cared for one another through all circumstances the same way, you were as open with one another. Your current relationship with all beings is not like that now, but you are *feeling it now.* In the beginning, remain with the best of your friends so you can become more adept at experiencing this feeling with regard to number two friends. And then work with number three friends based on that experience, without jumping right away to neutral people or enemies.

Of course this impinges on your mind: "I'm going to have to do this with neutral people; I'm going to have to be doing this with enemies." But hold back rushing on to neutral people and enemies. It's just too much of a stretch. After you actually enact the therapy by concentrating on friends to gain felt experience, you can move on to neutral people. Eventually, you will see them all as friends somewhere over the course of lifetimes, and since closeness predominates, that's the most important relationship.

Try to visualize each individual. If you're not good at visualizing, then just feel that the person is present in front of you. Then consider neutral people, not quickly, but over weeks. As you are able to cultivate the feeling of closeness more effectively, start with minor enemies. Keep going back in time as much as you can, doing it very slowly, because doing it slowly unties many knots. Think of your high school reunion. In time, you can go way back to grade school. Those enemies often loom larger in our minds. At first you don't *think* that they do, but then when you recall so-and-so who made fun of you because of whatever reason, you're back in that situation, and all the pain and humiliation come flooding back.

The implementation of this exercise is difficult, because we hold on to knotty experiences, but it isn't just a matter of letting go. It's a matter of transforming these experiences, thinking, "Just as my best friend is close and dear to me, so Priscilla Ferrin—with whom I competed for first in the class in the eighth grade—also was close and dear to me in a former life."

One of my own classmates in the sixth grade punched me in the jaw, and even though he broke his hand, I still bear a grudge. If I keep feeling he wronged me—if I remain hung up on the wrong—then my personality is defined in part in relationship to that scene. However, when now I see that person as close, as having been my best of friends, this undoes a good bit of the definition of myself. To see that person differently, I have to become different, too.

This can be disturbing, but it is also liberating. It could even be shattering, in a good sense, to break down these positions of friend, enemy, and neutral person. It won't change the fact that somebody deliberately stepped on your hand as you reached down to pick up a pencil in the third grade, but it will change the attitude you have toward that person. The fact that our personality forms out of our emotional involvement and in reaction to other people in such situations often makes it difficult to entertain a different relationship.

By meditating on people one by one, you feel the shock of change in your experience of that other person, and the mind is gradually transformed. Since the force of the meditation weakens from time to time, keep repeating the meditation. Eventually, it becomes second nature and even first nature.

PROBLEMS INTERRUPTING MEDITATION

There is a Tibetan story about a man who was cultivating patience in meditation. When he came out of meditation and went outside, someone bumped against him, and he got very angry and told the person off. The other person said, "You are not cultivating patience. Your meditation is no good at all."

The meditator said, "I will go back and cultivate a patience that none of you can even think of." He went back to his room and cultivated patience for a while.

One of his fellow meditators, who wanted to help him, thought he should test him. He defecated on a plate and went into the meditator's room, carrying the plate behind his back. He asked, "What are you doing?"

The meditator said, "I am cultivating patience."

"What kind of patience are you cultivating?"

"A patience such that, no matter what anyone does, I will not get angry."

"What did you say?"

The meditator repeated, very patiently, "A patience such that, no matter what anyone does, I will not get angry."

Then his friend put the plate in front of him and said, "In that case, eat shit."

The meditator said, "*You* eat shit!"

His friend picked up the plate and left without getting angry. The meditator reflected, "My friend did not get angry at all, but I got extremely angry. Perhaps he was just testing me." This test gave him a measure of what nonpatience is.

It's easy to explain the set of exercises for generating compassion but hard to do them, because set patterns in the mind are being disturbed. With regard to recognizing everyone as having been a friend, one possible difficulty could be that you have three number one friends—you can't make a difference between them. If you've got three number ones, don't let that stop you. Just consider that within the three, B was like A, and so forth. Then go through the rest of your friends one by one, proceeding to the least. Experience the shock, the reorientation of your attitudes that this recognition creates; don't let placement puzzles paralyze the process.

Or, you may find that rather than extending the strong feeling you have for your best friend, your relationship with that person weakens, your attitude turns to "*so* what": If friends were and will be enemies, then friends are useless! You might lose all sense of friendship, rather than extend it. So, give up keeping the friend-class so rigid, allowing the impact of the changeability of relationships to come home. Through this, you strengthen knowledge that relationships do not exist merely through their own force but have to be cultivated. Keep working at the meditation so that the greater friends do not become like the lesser, but, instead, the lesser become like the greater.

Or, you may have problems listing friends in any order, best to least, for any of several reasons. They may switch order over the course of the year, or they may change just because you are paying attention to them in meditation. In that case, give up trying to order them, and just proceed randomly among whoever appears to your mind, but don't rush to the most difficult.

Or, you might stray off to neutral people before going through all your friends. In this case, correct yourself, thinking, "I'm supposed to stick with friends." By returning to friends, the meditation will have more impact, because when considering friends, it is easier to gain the experience of equating two persons than it is when the meditation turns to neutral people. You need to get used to the experience of extending a sense of truly intimate closeness beyond usual boundaries so that this experience can assist with indifferent and cold categories of people.

Or, you might find that you use your meditation time to start to relive instances in a relationship. However, no matter how valuable and revealing reflection on the events of a particular relationship may seem, this blocks doing the exercise. It is said that when cultivating a certain virtue, the practice of another one is actually a distraction. Identify the distraction as a distraction, but don't get uptight about it. In this case, you are keeping yourself from undergoing transition to a new way of relating to others. Indeed, if you dwell on a particular relationship, you might gain a few interesting insights, but you will not make progress in the greater quest. Keep pen and paper next to your place of meditation, and when these enticing thoughts appear, write them down, along with "I'll think about it later." Otherwise you might get caught up wondering, "Gee, I haven't thought about that in a long time, that would be really fruitful to follow," and the value of the session would diminish or be nonexistent. If the insights seem just too good to allow you to return to the meditation, focus yourself by reflecting on the advantages of generating compassion, and use the notepad; you can come back to the topic later.

Or, you may get sidetracked noticing that someone is lower down the list than they had been in the past and get stymied over the reason. Don't worry about it; just continue. A balance has to be kept—you don't want to race through the meditation such that feeling is not evoked, and yet you don't want to spend time mulling over the details of a situation.

Or, you may be faced with too many people. Ten or fifteen, it's not so difficult to think they all want happiness and don't want suffering. But a hundred thousand? Should numbers bother us? They shouldn't, but sometimes they do. It requires more and more and more practice, until numbers make no difference.

MOVING TO NEUTRAL PERSONS AND ENEMIES

When you have identified that all friends are as close as the present best friend, turn to neutral persons. You will see how, if you have done the meditation of identifying friends as best friends well, identification of neutral persons as having been the most intimate of friends will be possible. Sometimes this just comes naturally. You may find that the exercise gets stronger as you move from one neutral person to the next, and there is a general opening up, so that as more individual neutral beings are taken to mind, there is no obstacle to deep recognition.

Then, when considering enemies, you will have to deal with obstacles—it's difficult to see enemies as having been friends. Practice an equanimity exercise: "Isn't it possible that this person wants happiness and doesn't want suffering, just like me?" "Isn't it possible that this person, like so-and-so neutral person, wants happiness and doesn't want suffering?" Just ask yourself these simple questions. You have to answer, "Well, yes"—and then notice your reaction—"but I can't stand the person."

Notice your feelings. The aim is not to suppress them, but to notice them and then reform them. Meditating on enemies as having been friends in a former lifetime is an excellent way to open up to the very depths of feelings of hatred. We're often

not open to them, they're so shatteringly awful. And so it takes
a sense of humor, it takes patience, it takes a long time to make
progress. "But what the heck, if I can make some progress with
neutral people, fantastic! Really!" Think of it. If you could bring
that into daily life, if you could experience a change of attitude
toward neutral people, even just in meditation, fantastic! Be
easy on yourself; adopt a long-term view: "If, after a few years,
I could bring this into my activities with neutral people, fantastic!" That takes the pressure off. There's no great failing if you
can't extend this sincerely on to enemies. Use the practice as a
chance to reveal some of your own baggage.

We usually discriminate strongly between someone who
intends to harm us and someone who doesn't. We think,
"That's all right; he didn't mean it"; or the person who has
harmed us can say, "Why do you blame me so much? I didn't
mean to." But we get really angry when we know people *mean*
to harm us. How could we possibly see such people as intimate, close, dear—as dear as our best of friends?

If you can retain a little compassion when people harm you
unintentionally, you have made progress. But if you retain it
when someone intends to harm you, you are really successful.
It's not that you think, "This person is marvelous; she's trying
to rob me," but you don't take these facts as reasons for hating
the person. You recognize the intention and put your wallet in
your front pocket. You take such measures, but the conditions
that prompted them no longer serve as reasons for hatred.

Our wish to love everyone and the actual attitudes we have
under pressure are in constant conflict. That's just the way

we are. We've been wandering in cyclic existence since begin-ningless time, because of desire and hatred, and it's going to take a lot of familiarization to change this. Be relaxed about it. Don't put pressure on yourself, thinking things like, "Oh, I'm a scumbag because I hate so deeply." Rather, try this attitude: "I have to admit it. As much as my ideals say I should love so-and-so-or at least be neutral—I have to face the fact that I don't." Go easy on yourself.

Treat yourself a little bit as if you're treating a child. The deep mind and the superficial mind aren't necessarily together. Although these reflective meditations have a big effect on the deep mind, the transformation is often slow, taking time.

✦ ✦ ✦

In sum, for me, the biggest obstacle in extending the medita-tion to enemies has always been an unwillingness to face just how much I hate the person. And how much I really do wish all sorts of horrible things on that other person. But, that's the way we are. It's not as if we were born with clean slates and thus the situation *ought* to be that the slate is clean. The sit-uation ought to be that the slate is *very* dirty. Beginningless lifetimes in cyclic existence, living in all sorts of weird ways, engaging in all sorts of counterproductive actions—of course we have deep-seated hatreds.

Begin with lesser enemies. The hard ones will come later.

VALUING OTHERS

THE DALAI LAMA'S
FAVORITE MEDITATION

THE DALAI LAMA is particularly fond of a meditation that promotes taking responsibility for others' well-being. Based on *A Guide to the Bodhisattva Way of Life* by the eighth-century Indian scholar-yogi-poet Shantideva, he calls for imagining a three-sided scene. **In meditation:**

1. **Imagine that you are your better, more relaxed, confident, and wise self in the middle looking at two sides in front of you to your left and right.**
2. **Then imagine your selfish self on one side: the person who, in a pushy way, is trying to get an earlier flight, or a piece of cake, or something like that—this person who's just thinking of herself or himself. Remember a recent incident or play-act a convincing instance of your nasty, cruddy self, thinking, "I, I, I," not your usual self, but a nasty, self-serving version.**

3. Across from your selfish self imagine a group of destitute persons—poverty-stricken or in pain.

Thus, in the middle looking at the other two sides is your wise, discriminating self. You look out to one side where your cruddy, selfish self is, utilizing any of a variety of examples:

1. Remember an incident when you were whining in self-pity about your own welfare, putting yourself totally, unreasonably ahead of everyone else. You were so wound up in your own thing that you couldn't notice somebody else's concern. It's awful. It's ugly.
2. Or, remember a situation when you unreasonably carried on, got angry.
3. Or, remember an instance of feeling selfish desire: You're in a store somewhere, you particularly want some item, you're getting overly fascinated with it.
4. Or, remember a time when you were greedily jealous. There's always someone among your acquaintances who makes more money for less work.

Then, on the other side, look at the group of destitute people. Sick. Living in poverty. Finding it difficult to get something to eat.

His Holiness asks the level-headed you in the middle to reflect on this fact: **"The selfish I on one side and the destitute ones on the other side equally want happiness and don't want suffering."** And then the question is: **Whom will I help?**

My selfish self, or the destitute people? Just imagine it. As the wise one, you are asking yourself, **"Which side am I going to help: the selfish one, groveling after her or his own welfare, or these destitute people?"**

The only conclusion is: **"There's only one of me; others are infinite in number, exemplified by five or ten destitute people. How could the welfare of this infinitely larger group not be more important?"**

In other circumstances, outside of such a graphic situation, it might seem that, in the abstract, self and other are equal: Self is one and other is one. They're both singular. But when, aided by this visualization, you actually consider what "other" is, it's composed of an incredible number of individual selves, individual I's.

But still, you might consider that, even in this scenario, you assume that the motivations of the "other" side could be just as self-cherishing as your own, and thus you could find no real qualitative difference between self and other. You might then be inclined to help all equally—including your own nasty, self-cherishing self. It strikes me that this is perfectly fine, as long as your nasty self amounts to just one and does not equal "other" in terms of number, who, quantitatively, are hugely different. Thus, if you are considering five people on the "other" side, then you should consider yourself one-sixth, not half.

Or, you might get stuck wondering whether this contemplation calls for helping others and not helping yourself at all. It seems to me that the win-win solution is to put the main emphasis on helping others, making altruism the motivation of self-improvement. What is being targeted here is the *feeling* of oneself being so exaggeratedly important in the process of becoming happy. *Everyone* wants happiness and doesn't want suffering.

Or, you think, "I *am* more important because I'm figuring this all out, and I'll be able to pass it on to ones who don't understand." I have found it fun to let this type of pride just be, not try to oppose it, but to think, "Even this sense of self-importance is for the sake of others." Think this over and over again, and pride, which usually serves to hide your inadequacies, disappears. The self-importance becomes hollow and fades. When I was interpreting for the Dalai Lama under the bright lights in front of large crowds, I found the situation brought a huge uplift in concentration—the communication of his message at that point depended on me. I enjoyed the challenge, enjoyed making myself inconspicuous but effective, enjoyed trying to make the task look effortless, enjoyed the open state of mind that I would need for adequate memory when he would talk for five minutes in Tibetan without break, enjoyed the interaction with him when, listening to my English, he would then repeat in Tibetan something I had missed. But I found that after leaving the stage, I longed to be back on it—the lights, the intensity, the attention. I found that it was getting so that I lusted after "the stage." I recalled stories of actors who could not stand themselves except when onstage and knew I had to figure a way out of this. After a while, this is what came to me: "May these feelings of intensity and so forth go for the benefit of those who are listening."

I thought this over and over, and it worked. I no longer lusted for the situation, but I accomplished this not by forcing myself to not want it, but by realizing that the whole activity was for the sake of others and by deeply feeling this realization in imagination—imagining strength entering into the bodies and minds of the audience. Any type of pride can be handled in the same way.

There are a lot of little things that we can do for others as we go about the day. Provide a cushion for somebody in your meditation group who has difficulty finding a cushion to sit on. Little actions mean a great deal to others. When the Dalai Lama visited the University of British Columbia, he had a meeting with the dean and a group of professors including an aged man who had come in just for this meeting with His Holiness. He was sitting down. When His Holiness entered the room, he tried to get up, although His Holiness was not very near. The fellow, a thin, very old man, was trying to get up to show his respect. All of us saw the great difficulty that he had getting up—such that he might fall down—and we felt in our hearts for him. However, the only one who moved quickly to help him was the Dalai Lama, who took hold of him and helped him up. His Holiness wasn't so full of himself as to think, "I'm here to receive these people."

So, it's the little things that count in valuing others. Making a decision to look to see how we can most effectively help those around *us*. With such a motivation, your activities have a true importance that is not self-centered. It's difficult to decide how much to give away, how much time to devote to others, but the basic motivation is clear enough, and it itself, on a day-to-day basis, unties a lot of problems.

Meditation:

Radiating Help

Once a sense of closeness with others has formed, you want to help them. A technique that is said to develop the capacity to be of actual benefit is to visualize helping others in imagination. **In meditation, visualize radiating beams of light, streams of ambrosia, out from your own heart. The beams enter into the minds and bodies of other beings. This helpful light, this beneficial substance, influences them such that as it penetrates flesh, blood, bone, mind, and so forth—streaming into the person's body and mind—it clears away problems and restores balance.**

Previously, we have been meditating that all beings want happiness and don't want suffering. Now, in this new phase of the meditation, we communicate this realization: Imagine, pretend, that this ambrosia radiates from your heart to others and enables them to reflect easily on the equality of all beings in this basic sense and to develop a feeling of closeness with all beings. Although this practice may not actually confer these abilities onto the people you are visualizing, you are enhancing the power of your own meditation by drawing other people into it, and seeing them meditate with the same purpose. Through this you help to clean up the psychic atmosphere.

The light is often described as five-colored—white, yellow, blue, green, and red—but this can be a bit too much to imagine.

Start the meditation with one person: Emit streams of light from your heart, and as the light enters, it puts that person's body at ease and affects the mind such that the person has the ability to reflect on the fact that all beings want happiness and don't want suffering and that all beings have been the best of your friends in a past life. The light beams give the person the ability to develop a feeling of closeness with all beings.

By imagining rays of ambrosia streaming from your heart to as many beings as you can imagine—including animals, and so forth—we reconnect to a sense of other-cherishing; we become imbedded in an attitude of making ourselves sources of help for others. As Nagarjuna says in his *Precious Garland*, using examples from a time before forests and so forth became restricted objects:

> If only for a moment make yourself
> Available for the use of others
> Just as earth, water, fire, wind, herbs,
> And forests [are available to all].

At the end of the *Precious Garland*, he recommends turning this aspiration into a wish repeated three times daily:

> May I always be an object of enjoyment
> For all sentient beings according to their wish
> And without interference, as are the earth,
> Water, fire, wind, herbs, and wild forests.

Meditation:

Taking Joy in Others' Success

It seems to me that when Shantideva, the eighth-century Indian master mentioned at the beginning of the chapter, says, "Though beings want happiness, they rush to suffering," our rush to suffering comes from deciding that we don't need to think about the fact that others want happiness and don't want suffering—that it's all right to look on others as things to be used in the process of gaining happiness. Usually, what we're trying to win is more happiness through money, friendship, fame, material goods, social status, and power, but the way we do it often undermines our chances for achievement in the short term. Furthermore, those attitudes double back on us later—we start complaining about others' having the very same attitudes toward us we had earlier toward them. We also gravely err when we mistake those things that were initially seen as means to happiness as happiness itself—more money in the bank becomes the goal.

Are we really this brutal? Sometimes greed is even a conscious credo. More often it is not raised to that level but is still our basic orientation, and if we dig deep enough, we find that it is our basic idea. It certainly is the way we act, and in this Buddhist system the way we act doesn't just come from instinct, but from fundamental ideas, such as "I'm first," which itself is built on the shaky foundation of failing to realize that others want happiness and don't want suffering. Ideas, not raw instinct, are at the basis of most behavior.

Joy is the wish that sentient beings retain whatever happiness they have, that they have happiness and liberation and never lose it. **In meditation, imagine people retaining their happiness, their wealth, their good looks, and so forth. Think of someone who is rich, and take delight in her or his having so much wealth. Or, apply the meditation to other situations—to people who have compassion, people who have various abilities—wishing that they retain these treasures.**

We often get caught up in competitiveness with others. Even if it's not our creed that we want others to fall behind or that we have to step over people, that is—in effect—what is happening. We're competing, and we want to win. In graduate school when I was learning Sanskrit, most in our class took it as a game, since the grammar is complicated, like chess. We would nudge each other: "Ah! You missed that," and carry on like that. We had a good relationship, and if someone else got the answer, we were quite pleased, but there was one student named Johnson who got ninety-nine or one hundred on a few tests, and the rest of us would wither in his presence. We began to feel, "May Johnson not do well! May he not figure this out!" We would think, "Poor old Johnson," unconsciously imagining that he would be sitting there stupidly; in our imagination the professor would ask, "What is the accusative dual of such and such?" and Johnson wouldn't know. This is what we were mixing our minds with; we were mixing our minds with stupidity. We were meditating it with respect to someone else, but it was *our* minds that were being mixed with it. We were destined to become more stupid in the end. Eventually, I realized this and made an effort to take joy in Johnson's fortune of doing particularly well. When he was asked a question in class, I consciously wished that he would know the answer immediately—in my imagination Johnson would out-Johnson Johnson. Wow he was quick! After the final exam, I asked the professor how I had done and how Johnson had done. I was shocked to learn that I had done better than Johnson and immediately expressed genuine sympathy for him, but my previous karma had been so bad that the professor looked me in the eye and said, "Don't try to fool me."

Joy is the opposite of jealousy. It is a way to turn away from merely serving your selfish side and value the multitude of others. It will make you a much happier person and enhance your relationships with those around you.

STEP THREE

REFLECTING ON OTHERS' KINDNESS

10

WAYS OTHERS ARE KIND

Meditation: Mama's Kindness

T HE NEXT STEP is to think in detail, to get a substantial, tangible appreciation, even a tactile feeling, of how each person was kind to you when he or she was your friend. That means you open up the scenario. In some sense, you've already done it, just by recognizing that number ten friend was just like number one friend two lifetimes ago. Thus, you've already gained a sense of his or her kindness to some degree, but in this step, you reflect: **"Just as I want to know how my friend is doing and just as she's wondering about me and we're looking forward to the good times ahead and remembering the good times gone by, so it was with number ten friend."**

Several of my Tibetan teachers have talked about the kindness of one's mother, how "my mother held me close to her flesh, rocking me to and fro on her ten fingers." Little babies and little children, when mothers pull the blanket up to their shoulders and tuck them in, feel, "Hmm, how nice!" Similarly, there's that feeling of running into the house to mother for protection. Little kids hug their parents' knees and feel cared for and safe. Evoke that childhood feeling.

If you are able to remember your own mother's kindnesses—if you are able to remember your deep feelings for her and many specific instances of what she did for you—or if you watch mothers now, or if you have a child of your own, you will see that a mother has to think about her child night and day, especially when it is an infant. If she stops thinking about the child even for an hour, it might die; if she stops thinking about it for ten or twelve hours, it may die; after twenty-four hours, it is close to dying.

We usually don't have to think about anyone for twenty-four hours; we can go about our business. But our mothers had to think about us almost twenty-four hours a day. Mothers often sleep lightly; when the child cries, Mother wakes up. This is hard for the mother, because the child cuts in on her time. She is tortured in her relationship to the child; though she loves the child, it is also clear—and this is hard to face—that she sometimes regrets that the child has taken the little freedom she once had. It can be hard to be with anyone who is that demanding.

Yet, hard as the mother's situation is, she does not give her child up. Kensur Lekden, abbot of the Tantric College of Lower Lhasa, made the shocking observation that, despite the suffering of childbirth, the mother "does not throw one away like feces, but cherishes and takes care of her child." This is obvious when you think about it, but we do not usually *realize* that we are here because our mothers did not give us up at some point in our childhood. His statement is graphic and meant to jar us.

Sometimes we feel, "My parents copulated; they conceived me; now, dammit, let them take care of me!" It is *their* fault that we have been born; let them take care of us! Out comes the hand, and they give a little money. But that is not enough; the hand comes right back out again. In Buddhist practice, however, you reflect that at the end of the previous lifetime your own consciousnesses—eye, ear, nose, tongue, body, and mental consciousnesses—collected at the heart. The consciousness may leave the body in many different ways, preferably upward or straight ahead, and it starts searching, so to speak, for a suitable place for rebirth. By its own predispositions it wants a certain place, and because our parents were copulating at that time, we obtained a human lifetime that is precious since it provides an opportunity to practice. That is a provocative Buddhist point of view. From this perspective, we are fortunate if we have a good rebirth and a good mother. It is certainly true that most of our mothers individually took care of us closely, with the exception of orphans and persons cared for by someone else.

Kensur Lekden said that we are much like helpless bugs when we are born. We just lie there, and despite wanting to move, even if we have presence of mind from our last lifetime, we cannot. We have a difficult time getting used to this new body. It is not trained. It is like someone who hurdled at age eighteen and at age forty-eight goes out to hurdle again, cracking knees and ankles on the hurdles. In the same way, though we had a body that was trained before, we can't use this untrained new one. Your mother feeds you; she changes your diapers; she has to do everything for you. Later, while she holds you in her arms, you put your fingers on her nose, and she says, "Nose." You reach for her eyebrow and stick your finger in her eye, and she says, "Eye." You put your finger on a tooth in her mouth, and she says, "Tooth." Because she does this day after day, you finally learn to talk. Your speech is built on her kindness. She seldom does this mechanically; it is amazing. If your own compassion is to become profoundly deep and strong, it helps to eventually awaken and vividly remember the strong relationship you had at the beginning of this life with your mother. By eventually taking her as the model of the helpful friend and applying your intimate knowledge of her closeness to every sentient being, the element of self-centeredness gradually falls away. We usually feel attachment to certain people and not to others, but when we apply this strong feeling to all sentient beings, the attachment fades.

In the previous step you recognized all sentient beings as mothers, as having been your mother in at least one former lifetime. Building on that, here in meditation you recognize that all of these beings have done these sorts of things for you. You need to be mindful of their kindness. Fill your mind with their kindness; become attentive to it. Mindfulness also means not forgetting.

Then, too, when you recognize how kind someone has been to you, you are using an ordinary worldly attitude to help keep you from responses of hatred. For instance, if someone gave me a grant with a blank check to form a team of translators of Tibetan thought, I would be more than extremely pleased. Now, if the person who gave me the money came by someday and gave me a hard time, I would feel a measure of restraint due to reflecting on the person's kindness. I would seek other means to work things out with the person. When you reflect how kind every person has been, there is that restraint to the point where, believe it or not, trained Buddhists will look at a fly or an ant walking across the table and think, "This is someone who bore me in her womb in a former lifetime, who took care of me."

If you watch how mothers take precautions for a child in the womb, it is clear that they do a great deal to help it. They eat nourishing foods and avoid harmful substances like coffee, alcohol, nicotine, and drugs. If you reflect on how such a mother takes care of the child in the womb and extend this reflection to all sentient beings, I think that because your field of awareness is no longer just a few sentient beings but is gradually expanding to more and more, you can reflect on the mother's kindness without doing it merely because *you* were helped. The staggering debt deflates your sense of exaggerated importance. The boil is pricked.

Start with number one friend and generate a sense that this person in a former lifetime is someone whose knees you grabbed as you would a parent's. In my case, it's my friend in Canada; I grabbed ahold of his knees in great delight. **Then move from friend to friend and to neutral people also.**

You may find it shocking that a neutral person is someone to whom, in a former lifetime, you ran up as a little child and from whom you took great comfort. A nice shock, and this opens up your heart. Enemies are more difficult, because we're so committed to maintaining distance, but when you succeed with neutral persons, move on to lesser enemies and then greater enemies.

You may find that it's difficult to generate the same degree of feeling with lower-level friends just because it's hard to imagine them reaching out and being comforting—it's not their style, it's not what they do. It's hard to imagine the guy at the lumber store reaching across the counter and comforting you, but in a former lifetime, when the guy at the lumber counter was your mother or father, and you were the little child, the situation was different. Still, the present situation may seem so frozen that it's impossible for that to have been the case; maybe it's just that he smells so different, compared to Mom.

Or, if you strayed too soon into considering an enemy, you might feel that it would be really difficult to trust that person in the way a child does when grabbing Mom around the knees. At that point you can appreciate the mental revolution that will have to occur before you can loosen up such that you could feelingly think, "It is sensible that a hundred lifetimes ago, if this person was my mother, she was as kind as Mom." We don't want to give up our fixated enemy-feeling—it's as if the person always was "enemy"; but that's just not reasonable.

As before, go back through your life, remembering people, but this time extend the warmth of appreciation for kindness to them. Going back through a lifetime this way will help reawaken memory. Gradually, you can remember crawling and experiences such as holding on to your mother—for instance, I clearly remembered that when my mother held me in her arms as a baby, I often played with an agate on the end of a zipper at the top of her dress. We had a different type of mind then. We say, "I was born on such and such a date," but we don't remember our birth. We say, "I lived in a certain town for five years," but we don't remember anything about it. One reason may be that we hold on to thoughts that we don't want to remember, bad thoughts about people. By developing this sense of appreciative closeness with people from your childhood, you can begin to loosen your grip on some of these buried feelings—and they can begin to loosen their grip on you.

To repeat: **Start with the best of friends and develop an appreciation of their kindness as if they were your mothers. Then move to lesser friends and then to neutral people. Then, to all the degrees of enemies.**

Meditation:
Appreciating the Nexus of Provisions Others Provide
Just as there are two ways of generating a sense of equanimity—one by acknowledging common aspirations to happiness and to be rid of suffering and the other by acknowledging the implications of rebirth in terms of relationships over the course of lives—so there are also two techniques to generate a sense of others' kindness. One, as just explained, is to reflect on the kindness of others to yourself in former lifetimes. The other

is: **In meditation, reflect on the value of the many goods and services that others provide.** In the latter case, appreciating kindness is not so much based on motivation but is a valuing of what is provided—for instance, the nexus of people who present us with a supermarket with all this stuff that we can buy and take home. Consider the trucker who delivers to the supermarket—the "kindness" of the truck driver. The truck driver may not look on it this way, but she provides; thus, this kind of appreciation means the *valuing* of something, regardless of motivation. I value my watch, but it doesn't have any motivation to help me—this is pure appreciation.

When you think of it that way, this nexus of people involved in providing a glass of water, all the people who are involved, *wow!* These are the types of thoughts that lead the Dalai Lama to say, "Kindness is society." Without kind motivation you don't have society, but also without recognition of this other type of kindness, you don't have society. You have one person fighting the other for the bottom line, thinking only of himself or herself, trying to outwit one another in order to rip one another off. We need to build up this type of appreciation; society will be healthier, we will be healthier, we will recognize the truth of the vast network on which we depend, in which we are imbedded. We will take more responsibility for one another, stopping, for instance, from trying to create consumer demand for a product that is actually dangerous. We will discover an ethic of commerce.

A Tibetan lama visiting us in Virginia made an intriguing observation about people in affluent societies. He said that

when you're affluent, you know where the next meal is coming from, you know where your roof will be tonight, where
your bed will be. If you don't find a good hotel room somewhere, you can go home! You have a house—it's not a *very* nice
house, but it's all right. And the refrigerator is stocked, and
your bed is hard, the way you like it. When you're affluent,
it seems you're not depending so much on other people. You
don't have to go out and beg. When you're begging, you're
dependent. If you don't have a roof over your head, you have
to look for shelter. You're dependent on somebody else to give
it to you.

So the affluent have a false sense of independence. A *false*
sense of independence. Why? Because all of the trappings of
their lives are dependent on others. All of them. Your money
is dependent on others. Imagine the nexus that allowed you to
make whatever money you have. The nexus that put up my
house. The nexus that allows me to have water when I turn on
my kitchen sink. It's all *thoroughly* dependent on others. But
because I'm affluent, I have more of a false sense of independence than people who aren't so affluent. And as the Tibetan
lama said, *once* you have this stronger sense *of* self-sufficiency,
you have more self-cherishing.

And then, the real blast was that he said that with more self-
cherishing you have more self-pity! It was like being hit in the
chest with a battering ram. With more self-cherishing, there's
more self-pity: "All the terrible things that are happening to
me. This is going wrong, and that's going wrong, and I don't
have this, and I don't have that." The more independent you

are, the more you end up being self-pitying about what you *don't* have. Very interesting. "This is going wrong, and that's going wrong. This person's against me, that person's against me. The world's against me. I can't seem to get ahead. Blah blah blah." Whereas if you're poor, if you're struggling, that's the situation you're in, and you're craftier about how to deal with it. You're not lamenting so much about what you don't have. It's just the condition that you're in.

So, to overcome this false sense of independence, we need to reflect on how dependent we are. How my situation of having a house and nice acres of land out in the Blue Ridge, how I've got everything sort of set up, it's *all* dependent.

Several years ago, when the Dalai Lama was lecturing in Santa Barbara in a university gymnasium, there was a large crowd. He was talking in English about how his own fame was dependent on newspaper and television reporters. He wasn't even owning his own fame! True enough, fame arises in dependence upon other people; somebody else has to think, "WOW!"

Step Four

Returning Kindness

RECIPROCATING ON
YOUR OWN TERMS

W HAT DO YOU think would be the chief obstacle in recognizing that each individual person has been kind to you? In my case, I was afraid of having to return the kindness, because then I'd be under the control of these people. I didn't want to do what my parents wanted me to do, although they gave me a lot of slack—I left college after my first year, went to the woods of Vermont, went to Tahiti, all on my own with whatever cash I earned. I didn't fit into the upper-middle-class community where we lived. I didn't want their control; the lifestyle they were pushing on me was completely unappealing. Therefore, I refused to recognize their kindness.

However, assuming a debt with respect to every sentient being differs greatly from having a debt to a few. **In this meditation, you start with friends, then neutral persons, and then enemies and contemplate: "I will return the debt of kindness that I have with this person through helping her or him**

achieve happiness." It is easy to determine that the response to all sentient beings' kindness cannot be to do everything they want, since, with so many people, what they want from you would be at cross-purposes. You cannot even do everything your mother of this lifetime wants you to do, though you know her advice is, for the most part, motivated by kindness. If, like me, you go to India or Tibet, the whole trip is a time of worry for her—dysentery, liver failure, kidney failure; I'm sure she can imagine many things I wouldn't think of.

"Why don't you take some dysentery pills with you?"

That makes sense.

"Why don't you take some pills to purify the water?"

That makes sense.

"Why don't you take a big thermos? You could use it to put water in."

"I'll take a small thermos."

"No, you need a big one. What would you do if you got on the train and it broke down?"

What would I do? I don't know. But how much can I carry? It doesn't necessarily follow that if I recognize her worry as kindness, I have to carry that big thermos.

Those who help us—our parents, for instance—often attain power over us for that very reason: "Do as I say because I have helped you." Thus, for some, it becomes almost a mental habit to refuse to recognize those who have helped us, because they otherwise would attain some power over us. Still, we know we should return their many kindnesses. That is one reason why the practice of reflecting, "This person has helped me in many intimate ways and thus I must do something in return," gets to be uncomfortable, but when it is extended to more and more beings, we have to find a way of intending to return their kindness without coming under their misguided influence. The influence of the friend, the one who has helped, sometimes is not salutary. For instance, if you decide that such practices of altruism are worthwhile, you may find opposition from those who have helped you, and you may find that what they want you to do is unsuitable. You don't have to change these people; they will have their own time to change. But there is no need to change your style of behavior just because someone who helped you is urging you to do this or that. Someone who knows what should be done, whose decision is sufficiently strong, can seek to return others' kindness and not necessarily have to do as they say. Such a person is unusually strong.

Every sentient being has been one's mother. Yet one cannot do everything all those sentient beings want. There are so many of them, and they want such contradictory things. Besides, to fulfill what they temporarily want may not be the best way to help them. The greatest of all ways to return their kindness is to help them become free from all suffering and to assist in the process of becoming liberated from cyclic existence and attaining the bliss of Buddhahood. It is important to realize here in the step of developing an intention to return others' kindness that acknowledging a debt does not mean that you must do what they say. Otherwise, you might hold back from the truth of their attentive care.

Once you are intimate with all sentient beings, how can you bear to see them suffer? As the late Kensur Lekden said in his often stark and jarring way, if you saw that your own mother had fallen into a ditch and broken her leg and you didn't help her out of the ditch, who would? Would you stand by the ditch, looking down at your own mother, and say, "Oh, so she broke her leg," and pass on? If her own son or daughter would do that to her, who would help her? You would jump in and get her out right away.

Such a sense of readiness to respond is what the exercise of developing a wish to return others' kindness is aimed at generating. Indeed, when you develop an intention to return kindness to such a vast number of people, it is as if you're coming under the control of all of them. In Tibetan, the notion of being under the control of others is reframed, just slightly, so that it takes on a positive meaning in the context of compassion; it's called coming under the other-influence of compassion. Compassion may seem to be weak, but I was in the weak position of not recognizing my parents' kindness. With recognition of debt for theirs and others' kindness and recognition that I couldn't possibly do everything that everybody wanted me to do, I myself had to decide how to repay everyone. This realization can open up the possibility of stronger recognition of the similarity of others, the closeness of others, and with that comes strength. This kind of debt brings strength, not weakness. Thus, people who feel a debt to all sentient beings are, in a sense, under their influence in that they are committed to their welfare, but they attain more freedom through their attitude. You are weak if you cannot feel that dependence, if you are afraid of it.

Let me recount a story about my hometown, an incident involving a gay boy that I heard about several years after I left the town. The boy had long hair, and a football player beat him up, banging his head repeatedly against a stone wall. The gay boy's mother called up the football player's mother and apologized to her for her own son! How could I possibly wish to return her other, true kindnesses to me when she was my friend in past lifetimes if I thought that I had to conform to her warped attitude that blinded her love for her son? There would be no way! However, that is not the point. Her past caring for me does not require that I affirm all of her present attitudes. I must make my own decisions on how to respond to her earlier kindnesses; conformity to her present rigidity and blindness would help no one. I can start by wishing that she generate the realization that her son wants happiness and does not want suffering. It is not easy to respond so sensibly to such ignorant cruelty.

We often think of friendliness as a gift, either an outright gift from genes or from something that the person brings from the previous lifetime. That sometimes may be the case, but I have found that among Tibetan teachers, this "gift" of friendliness is a matter of engaging in just this kind of practice patiently, over a long period of time. Taking it to heart. Not letting it go by as just one of the teachings repeated by rote. Being willing to keep working on it and facing difficulties, such as when encountering beggars, or the person down the street, or the person sitting next to you. But the trick is to work initially with people with whom it's easier to accomplish. Be clever about building up experience with easier people. You might think you're avoiding the more difficult. But really you're building up experience so that there's some force of mind, such that when you get to the more difficult, you have a chance of making a little bit of progress and you're not just slapped down by your own habitual emotions, thinking: "I can't do this. It's not me." What's me? What's me is just what I've been used to for so long.

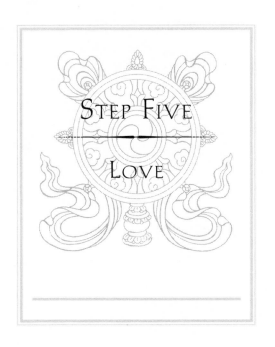

STEP FIVE

LOVE

MEDITATING LOVE

CULTIVATION of a sense of closeness with others—
along with the enhancements of reflecting on their
kindness and developing a wish to return that kindness—naturally and easily leads to love, which is the coun-
terpart of compassion. Whereas love is the felt thought "How
nice it would be if this person had happiness and the causes of
happiness," compassion is the felt thought "How nice it would
be if this person were free from suffering and the causes of suffering!" If everyone had happiness and the causes of happiness, it would be nice—wouldn't it?

Love for close persons and spiritual love are not completely
different, but spiritual love is cleansed of partisanship and bias
by being directed to all sentient beings. Ordinary, biased love
that we feel only for particular persons—which is often built
merely on the fact that another person brings us pleasure—
easily turns into consternation or flips to hatred when the person does not provide the familiar pleasure. Bitter arguments
erupt, but even they can flip back to loving tenderness when
the reciprocal relationship of pleasing is restored.

The meditation of spiritual love, however, is dramatically different in that its field has to be extended toward every being of every type. To accomplish this, the generation of love in meditative practice again has to begin with specific persons by considering individually all the people you have been remembering in the previous exercises and any new ones that might come to mind. Start with friends because they are easy to love; then pass to persons toward whom you are neutral and finally to enemies.

In meditation, imagine your best friend and think: "How nice it would be if this person had happiness and the causes of happiness!" This attitude is easy to feel with respect to your best friend because you already care intimately for that person's feelings. **Then, using that person and the feeling generated as a model, pass to the next level friend: "How nice it would be if this person had happiness and the causes of happiness!"** You probably will not feel it so intensely, but you can cause the intensity of the wish for this person to have happiness and the causes of happiness to increase through three steps: **Reflect on (1) how this person, just like your best friend, also wants happiness and does not want suffering; (2) how this person, over the course of lives, has also extended great kindnesses; and (3) the fact that you want to return that kindness. Try superimposing the image of your best friend on this friend, highlighting one and then the other, back and forth, until the intensity of the wish increases. Continue this exercise with each of your friends.**

Then pass on to neutral persons: "How nice it would be if

this person at the supermarket checkout had happiness and the causes of happiness!" It can be a real shock to see your attitude change from one of indifferent neglect to a strong sense of the person's humanity. Practice with many, many neutral persons individually such that you gain experience with the process. It is most enlivening, clearing away clouds of disconnectedness, confusion, and self-centeredness.

With this experience, you can pass on to the varying levels of enemies, beginning with the least. Practice until you can *feel this wish* as strongly as you feel it for the best of your friends. At first, you just say the words, but the feeling develops: "How nice it would be if this person had happiness and the causes of happiness!" Work gradually. Frequent meditation will dissolve layers of recalcitrant ill will. Eventually, someone else's intent to harm will no longer serve as a reason for hatred.

CAUSES OF HAPPINESS

It's important to think about the causes of happiness. In Buddhism the causes of happiness are often depicted as avoiding ten nonvirtues, or negative actions, and adopting ten virtues, or positive actions, opposite to the nonvirtues.

By extension, virtues also are the predispositions these activities establish in the mind.

All ten virtues are founded on concern for others. As the Dalai Lama frequently says, "Buddhist ethics can be summed up in two statements: If you are able to help others, then help;

three physical nonvirtues to be avoided	*three physical virtues to be adopted*
Killing	Refraining from killing, and sustaining life
Stealing	Refraining from stealing, and being generous with resources
Sexual misconduct	Refraining from forced and hurtful sexual conduct, and promoting good relations

four verbal nonvirtues to be avoided	*four verbal virtues to be adopted*
Lying	Refraining from lying, and telling the truth
Divisive talk	Refraining from divisive talk, and promoting harmony
Harsh speech	Refraining from harsh speech, and speaking lovingly
Senseless chatter	Refraining from senseless chatter, and speaking to a purpose

three mental nonvirtues to be avoided	*three mental virtues to be adopted*
Illegitimate acquisitiveness	Refraining from illegitimate acquisitiveness, and cultivating joy in others' prosperity
Harmful intent	Refraining from harmful intent, and cultivating helpfulness
Wrong views	Refraining from wrong views, and learning correct views

if you are not able to help, at least do not harm." These two are
the guiding principles, and a powerful way to internalize these
principles and the ten virtues that flow from them is to cultivate compassion through the steps that are being explained
here.

Cultivating realization of equanimity—the similarity of oneself and others in wanting pleasure and not wanting pain—
undermines impulses to kill, steal, or engage in coercive sex.
Cultivating knowledge of the closeness of others over the
course of lifetimes and a wish to reciprocate their kindnesses
weakens the pull to deceive, speak divisively, bark out harshly,
or just rattle on senselessly. Cultivating joy in others' favorable
qualities—youthfulness, beauty, wealth, or fame—relieves the
pangs of the jealousy of wishing that they lose what they have
and wanting it for yourself. Cultivating a wish for others' happiness and causes of happiness holds you back from slipping
into wishing them harm. Developing wisdom (explained in
subsequent chapters on compassion) slowly undermines distorted perspectives. Thus, the practices involved in developing
compassion eventually make the ten virtues natural reflexes
and bring real happiness.

If a person has these *causes* of happiness, she can stay happy,
whereas if she is just experiencing happiness for the moment,
merely enjoying the fruits of previous causes, as is the case
with   purchases from a paycheck, her situation easily turns
into pain and sadness. Thus, love is not just the wish that
others have happiness; the wish must also include that others
have the causes of happiness—the ten virtues.

Meditation:

Three Degrees of Love

Buddhist texts speak of three degrees of love. The first is the one described at the beginning of the chapter: **"How nice it would be if this person had happiness and the causes of happiness!"** The next degree of love is stronger: **"May this person have happiness and the causes of happiness!"** The force of thought is stronger because it is not worded in the hypothetical "if," but in the form of an intended, or wished for, future. **This second level of love is meditated in the same way as the first level, beginning with your best friend, then lesser friends, then neutral persons, then lesser enemies, and finally greater enemies, but with the felt attitude: "May this person have happiness and the causes of happiness!"** It is more mentally active, in a sense projecting your wishes into the midst of the workings of world society.

The second level cannot be practiced merely as a rote repetition of the first with a slight change of words. Rather, analytical meditation is needed; you need to reflect again on:

+ Your similarity with the other person (equanimity)
+ How the person has helped you during certain periods over the course of lifetimes or through providing helpful services in society (reflecting on kindness)
+ How you should reciprocate that kindness (developing an intention to return kindness)

Through reinstating the previous analysis, you heighten your mental state so that the wish, "May this person have happiness and the causes of happiness," has particular force. Once that force has been achieved, remain with that attitude in meditation—feeling it, letting it seep through your consciousness. Do not immediately move on to the next step; this is called stabilizing meditation, because you are stabilizing in the state that has been produced.

The procedure of analytical meditation is to move through a series of reflections in order to heighten perception and feeling, but once that perception and feeling have been gained, stay with that level. It may be so strong that you might be led to think it will last forever, but it will not; you have not yet reached the level where meditative stabilization feeds off of meditative stabilization—you are merely getting a taste of such a helpful, higher state. So, stay with the state in stabilizing meditation, and as soon as it weakens, return to analytical meditation to restore and intensify it, and then switch back to stabilizing meditation. This is how to gain and retain the impact of meditative insight.

The third level of love is unusual; it is the attitude: "I will cause this person to have happiness and the causes of happiness." It is practiced as above, beginning with your best friend, then lesser friends, passing on to neutral persons, then lesser enemies, and finally considering greater enemies. Utilizing all the techniques that you have developed in the practice of meditation—ranging from overcoming laziness through reflecting on the advantages of a concentrated mind to how to switch between analytical and stabilizing meditation— begin again the process of heightening love. This time you are making the highly unusual step of committing yourself to

each person's harrowing journey to real happiness—to bringing about the happiness of others no matter how many eons it
might take. This is true heroism.

During my first year in graduate school at Wisconsin, where
I went after five years at the Tibetan and Mongolian monastery
in New Jersey, a professor of psychiatry somehow heard I was
there and called, asking if I would stop by his office to talk
about learning how to meditate. We had a friendly relationship from the start. "How much do you charge?" he asked. I
answered, "How much do you charge your patients? That's the
amount." He told me, and we began meeting once a week. But
when it came to explaining the type of meditation we would
be doing, I immediately decided that it would be better not to
explain that we were aiming at becoming so close and respon-
sible for others that we would seek enlightenment in order to
free everyone from suffering and the causes of suffering and
join everyone with happiness and the causes of happiness. So I
suggested that instead of talking about the journey, we take it.
We immediately sat on the floor of his office, imagined individuals we knew, and began the first exercise in equanimity, "Just
as I want. . . , so . . ." We would share our experiences and move
on to the next meditation. After several weeks, he said, "I think
we probably should reduce the number of meetings." Knowing that persons in therapy usually make this move when they
are about to advance, I immediately countered, "Let's make it
twice a week." Over the course of the year we had a marvelous
time probing our feelings about the cast of characters in our
lives and moving ahead in the exercises. Ultimately, we were

sitting there on the floor of his office cultivating a commitment to joining all with happiness and freeing all from suffering. We were dazzled.

VALUE OF ENEMIES:
SITUATIONS FOR ADVANCEMENT

The greatest problems in developing love are our enemies, the most unyielding blocks to becoming unbiased. We feel that enemies are to be avoided as detriments to happiness. However, the Dalai Lama repeatedly says that enemies are to be valued because they provide situations for advancement. They don't have any motivation to help you advance, but they furnish such a situation. There are all sorts of things that don't have any motivation to help but provide us valued opportunities. For instance, a farmer has a field that has rich soil and good produce; the field doesn't have a motivation to help, but the farmer values it. I value my watch; I take care of it.

The Dalai Lama, speaking from his own experience, presents an interesting point of view for reevaluating enemies. During lecture tours, he goes through an argument such as, "Only with respect to other sentient beings can one practice patience, and if nobody is angry at you, how can you practice patience? Therefore, enemies are valuable."

The difficulties in our lives provide opportunities for the practice of love—for giving us a realistic appraisal of how close or far away we are from universal love. How else do we find out how deep our practice is except by being confronted by such situations? They provide glimpses into our own character to reveal how superficial our practice has been so far, thereby highlighting opportunities for deepening its application.

The great Indian scholar-yogi Nagarjuna gives advice about enemies that at first seems underhanded. He says that in order to overcome an enemy, you should cultivate your own good qualities such that your enemy will be upset:

> Even if you seek to harm an enemy,
> You should remove your own defects and cultivate good qualities.
> Through that you will help yourself,
> And the enemy will be displeased.

Rather than bad-mouthing an enemy, Nagarjuna suggests that we cultivate our own good qualities, thereby generating consternation in the enemy. At first blush, the technique seems just too obviously self-serving! However, the main point is that if you're going to be bad, be wisely bad. The Dalai Lama frequently gives the joking (but serious) advice that if you're going to be selfish, be wisely selfish—which means to love and serve others, since love and service to others bring rewards to oneself that otherwise would be unachievable. The worst way to attempt to gain happiness is to remove enemies from the count of humans and concentrate only on yourself; enemies must be kept within, or returned to, the count of humans.

Nagarjuna speaks of one moment of love as creating tremendous power:

Even three times a day to offer
Three hundred cooking pots of food [to monastics]
Does not match a portion of the merit
In one instant of love.

Though [through love] you are not liberated,
You will attain the eight good qualities of love—
Gods and humans will be friendly,
Even [nonhumans] will protect you,

You will have mental pleasures and many [physical]
    pleasures,
Poison and weapons will not harm you,
Without striving you will attain your aims,
And be reborn in the world of Brahma.

When I was a young child, my oldest brother—twelve years
older than I—had a variety of ways to torture me. One was
to come to my bedroom in the morning and, after tickling me
into peals of happiness during which I would retreat under
the blanket, smother me with that very blanket until I burst
into tears. Another was when I was walking down the front
stairs: the soles of my shoes were made of smooth leather such
that, small as I was, I found it difficult to manage the slippery
wooden steps. The railings, however, stretched up to the banis-
ter, which was too high for me to reach, so I would grab hold of
a railing and move down step by step. My brother came round
from the living room to the bottom of the steps and whispered

an insult about anyone who had to hold on to railings. So I let go and tumbled down the stairs. In my own stubbornness from fear of his chiding, I did this many, many times. I will stop there with recounting the tortures. But many years later, after I had become very strong and agile in prep school wrestling, when we were outside one day, we both understood that I was now the stronger one, and he took off running. I caught up with him; he put his arms to his sides and motioned for me to go ahead and punch him. I started to raise my arms but stopped—when the opportunity came, I just didn't want to get back.

Love is about finding something pleasant in everyone. It can't be external appearance, or what the person is engaged in at the moment; it has to be just the fact that this is a sentient being who wants happiness and does not want suffering and who has been the best of friends at some time in the limitless past. A Tibetan definition of love is that the person pleasantly comes to mind (*yid du 'ong ba*). Rather than pushing people away, you experience a core similarity and closeness in them that makes you receptive to their basic being, regardless of the problem— regardless of how distorted their current attitudes and behavior are. That's how strong spiritual love is.

I continually saw this loving commitment played out in small and big ways in the Dalai Lama's daily life. In Los Angeles a group of us, including Richard Gere, Harrison Ford, and Melissa Mathison (the writer of *E. T.* and *Kundun*), was passing through a hotel kitchen with the Dalai Lama as a shortcut to a fund-raising dinner. His Holiness looped his arm through mine and leaned on me; it was about six-thirty in the evening, and he had been going since four-thirty in the morning. He whispered, "I'm tired." Recalling how Bobby Kennedy was shot in the kitchen of a Los Angeles hotel and guessing that the group of us with him were all flashing to this, I said, "It's no wonder," all the while looking around. As we passed by a big steel table where five or six cooks were, His Holiness stepped toward them and, looking at them, smiled. They offered no response except to stare at him coldly, but he gave them a bigger smile, still with no response, and then he laughed a little from his belly, whereupon they broke out into smiles and laughter. Their sense of distance was gone, and his own tiredness was cleared away. At the dinner he gave an especially long talk in English, first teasing everyone at length about the disparity between how nice everything looked on the outside and what the inside of their medicine cabinets contained. Then he described in greater length the dire situation in Tibet due to the extremely brutal communist Chinese invasion and how a loving response that takes into account how the fault lies with the oppressors' attitude and not the basic person is needed.

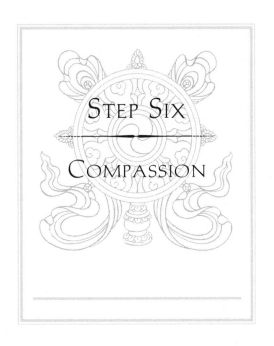

STEP SIX

COMPASSION

OVERVIEW OF COMPASSION

C OMPASSION IS the heartfelt wish that sentient beings be free from suffering and the causes of suffering. The Indian scholar-yogi Chandrakirti, one of the most renowned sources for Buddhist practice in Tibet, praises compassion as being important throughout spiritual practice:

> Mercy alone is seen as the seed
> Of a Conqueror's rich harvest,
> As water for development,
> And as a ripened state of long enjoyment.
> Therefore at the start I praise compassion.

Mercy and compassion are the same. Chandrakirti praises compassion because it is the root cause of Buddhas. When he praises the cause, he is implicitly praising the effect, but he is mainly emphasizing that Buddhahood arises from compassion.

Compassion is called the seed because it is the beginning of the path for bodhisattvas—those dedicated to becoming fully enlightened to be of benefit to other beings. Bodhisattvas are distinguished from other Buddhist practitioners in that they have *great* compassion, in that they themselves will free all sentient beings from suffering and the causes of suffering. They also have *great* love, in that they themselves will join all sentient beings with happiness and the causes of happiness.

The seed is what begins the harvest. Without the seed, one cannot have the fruit. The source of Buddhahood is compassion. Though wisdom is required for the attainment of Buddhahood, unshakable compassion is the differentiating factor. Other types of practitioners must also understand the final nature of reality in order to attain their respective, but lower, types of enlightenment. Thus, compassion alone is the seed of Buddhahood.

Compassion is also like the water that rains down and grows the potential harvest, once the seed has been planted. Compassion moistens the mental continuum; through the continued practice of compassion, the bodhisattva's progress advances. In the state of Buddhahood, it has ripened; it is like a matured fruit for enjoyment by others in that only a fully mature compassion causes enlightened beings to appear to others to help them in whatever form is suitable to their needs.

What would it be like for you or for somebody else—say, a Tibetan nun or monk—to have an aspiration to free every sentient being throughout the multiple universes from suffering and to join every one of those sentient beings with happiness? Free all sentient beings? You may think this is crazy. It should strike you as almost madness. One person, one tiny person, takes upon himself or herself the burden of freeing everyone in even a city from suffering; if this does not strike you as mad, it is not appearing to your mind.

There are people who have such wishes. Such a person sees a sentient being as someone for whom he or she will become enlightened in order to help that person free himself or herself from suffering and attain happiness. Not only that, such a person extends his or her mind throughout all of space and imagines sentient beings everywhere, and these sentient beings are like his or her own friends. What would it be like to be such a person?

TYPES OF COMPASSION

There are three types of compassion. The first is compassion seeing suffering beings, qualified by the suffering of misery, the suffering of changeability, and the suffering of being caught in a process of contaminated conditioning. The second is compassion seeing evanescent beings, qualified by impermanence and insubstantiality. The third is compassion seeing empty beings, qualified by not having any apprehensible signs of inherent existence. The example used for beings qualified by suffering is a bucket in a well, tied to a wheel or windlass. The example used for beings qualified by impermanence is the reflection of a moon in rippling water. The example used for beings qualified by not having any apprehensible signs of inherent existence is the reflection of the moon in clear water.

There are also three forms of compassion according to subjective aspect—what the compassion consciousness itself is doing. The first is the perspective, "How nice it would be if all beings were free from suffering and the causes of suffering!" The second is the perspective, "May they be free from suffering and the causes of suffering!" The third is the perspective, "I will free them from suffering and the causes of suffering."

These aspects of compassion point to our deepest nature, and yet, because we are conditioned otherwise, they will appear to be unnatural when first practiced. However, meditation, being a process of familiarization, gradually clears away the obstacles. Let's turn to techniques for cultivating these types of compassion in the next three chapters.

14

COMPASSION SEEING
SUFFERING BEINGS

C HANDRAKIRTI PAYS HOMAGE to three particular kinds
of compassion. The first is called compassion seeing
suffering beings, because prior to cultivating wishes
for persons to be free from suffering and the causes of suffering, you need to reflect on the dire condition of being trapped
in cyclic existence.

He describes the process of cyclic existence—birth, aging,
sickness, and death—as stemming from ignorance and nour-
ished with attachment and grasping. This means that our sense
of self is exaggerated beyond what actually exists, and based on
this exaggeration, we are drawn into many problems. Once the
"I" is exaggerated, the "mine"—the things that are owned by
the I, mind and body—also becomes exaggerated, overblown.
We say, "my mind": something we use. It is true that body,
mind, hand, head, house, clothing, are "mine"; they do belong
to us, but we have an exaggerated sense of owning them.

Conceiving of a concretely existing I and then conceiving

of concretely existing mine, we enter into desire and hatred and are drawn down into cyclic existence—battered, bruised; falling down into lives as animals, hungry ghosts, hell-beings; being reborn again in higher lifetimes as humans, demigods, and gods. Every sentient being throughout all of space is suffering this way. I am suffering this way. This is to be thought first with respect to yourself, realizing your own state—how many headaches, how many illnesses you have, and if you do not have many illnesses now, how many you are bound to have in the future, how pleasure turns into pain, how we are caught in a contaminated process of conditioning.

Meditation:
A Bucket Battered in a Well
Chandrakirti presents a vivid example for contemplation of how sentient beings suffer:

> Homage to that compassion for transmigrating beings
> Powerless like a bucket traveling in a well
> Through initially adhering to a self, "I,"
> And then generating attachment for things, "This is mine."

In meditation, imagine a bucket traveling in a well, tied to a wheel, controlled by the operator of the mechanism, going down into the dark depths and up to the brighter top over and over again, being drawn up with difficulty and strain and easily descending back down to the bottom, involved

in a process the order of which is difficult to determine, and while clattering against the sides of the well, being battered and broken.

Contemplate: Just as the bucket is tied by a rope to the wheel, so we are bound by past actions contaminated by the afflictive emotions of lust, hatred, and ignorance. Just as the turning of the wheel—be it a water wheel with many buckets strapped to it or a windlass with one bucket tied to it—depends upon a person operating it, so our wandering in cyclic existence depends upon consciousness. Just as the bucket travels down to the bottom of the well and up to the top, so we travel among the stations of cyclic existence, being born over and over again as hell-beings, hungry ghosts, animals, humans, demigods, and gods. Just as the bucket descends easily in the well but is difficult to draw upward even with hard work, so our own tendencies of mind— our lust, hatred, and ignorance—are such that we are easily drawn down into lower states of existence, but to change the momentum of this movement to lower states and move toward higher ones we must make a great deal of effort. Just as with the turning of a water wheel or the wandering of the bucket in the well, the temporal order of what happens first, in the middle, and last is difficult to determine, so our afflictive emotions, actions, and sufferings mutually lead to each other, making it impossible to determine in general the order of these three. Just as the bucket is battered against the walls of the well, so we are battered by the sufferings of mental and physical pain, the suffering that occurs when pleasure leads to pain, and the suffering that comprises the mere fact of being caught in an afflicted process of conditioning. Powerlessly, sentient beings are wandering among bad states and better states.

When, through analytical meditation, a vivid sense of their pain is manifest to you, within a sense of their closeness as cultivated in the earlier steps, take your best friend to mind. **Contemplate: "How nice it would be if this person were free from suffering and the causes of suffering!"** When a strong sense of compassion arises, stick with this feeling in stabilizing meditation. Then, pass on to your next best friend, and repeat the process in brief form if you are successful and with more detail if further cultivation is necessary. Continue this way through neutral persons, lesser enemies, and finally stronger enemies. By consistently making progress the walls of bias gradually disappear, and the possibility of the truly universal is glimpsed.

Using the same format, in meditation cultivate the second level of compassion: "May they be free from suffering and the causes of suffering!" When you succeed with that, move to the third level of compassion. **Using the same procedure, contemplate: "I will free them from suffering and the causes of suffering."** Here you are assuming on yourself the burden of freeing each and every being from pain. Although no one has to do this alone, you develop such strength of will that you can imagine that if you had to accomplish this alone, you would. Progress toward such an attitude endows you with more patience, more endurance, more tolerance. The threshold of anger moves further and further away.

As you go through the process of the meditations, you will undergo sometimes heartwarming and sometimes shocking changes that will foster the sense that dramatic changes can be accomplished through long-term practice. Stay with it; the description has many steps, but only one step—only one contemplation—is done at a time, and each one of them is an opening to a new orientation.

Through first reflecting in meditation on the example of the bucket in a well, vividly feeling it, and then replacing it with yourself—"This is the type of suffering I am undergoing"— you recognize your own suffering. When you recognize the extent of your own suffering, you generate a wish to get out of cyclic existence, and when you apply that understanding to other beings who are viewed as intimate and close through the previous meditations, compassion is generated. The mere perception of others does not generate compassion. If you do not see them as undergoing suffering and as being close, why would you have commiseration for them?

COMPASSION SEEING
EVANESCENT BEINGS

THROUGHOUT HISTORY brilliant poets, sometimes late in their life, have written about how all things are impermanent; yet it often takes a whole lifetime to realize this. Indeed, it is true that youth fades, and it fades fast. Older people often say, "You will be old, too," and you think, "Maybe in another twenty years or so." Their point is not just that you too will be old but that you take false pride in youth, thinking that it will last longer than it does. "I myself was young," they say, "and it seems only a few days ago. Now look at me." Their point is that there is no gulf between youth and age; you are youthful, and then you turn around and ten years have gone. They are saying that you are solidifying the future, thinking, "I am going to do this; I am going to do that." Their message is that the future is not solid.

Why are we surprised when someone dies? We know that everyone has to die. We know that we are to die. Still, there is surprise. Our amazement at the rapid passage of time indicates something wrong with the way we see things. There has to be exaggeration in our perception; otherwise, why are we so astonished when things change?

Meditation:
The Reflection of the Moon in a Rippling Lake
Besides compassion seeing sentient beings—that is, sentient beings as qualified by suffering—Chandrakirti speaks of another type of compassion: compassion seeing evanescent beings. He says:

> Homage to that compassion for transmigrating beings
> Seen as evanescent,
> Like a moon in rippling water.

Chandrakirti uses the image of the reflection of the moon in rippling water. **In meditation, imagine a lake; there is a light breeze, and the water is covered by ripples. It is a cloudless night. A full moon is reflected in the water, and notice how the reflection of the moon in the water shimmers, flickers. Then switch to a person and see that person as evanescent, transitory, impermanent like the shimmering reflection of a moon in rippling water.**

Usually, we see the moon as just the moon; we see it one night and expect to see it the next with a sense that it is somewhat constant. In this meditation, however, we see the reflection of the moon shimmering. We don't see the reflection of the moon as a solid thing but as something in motion, in constant change. Since it is rippling in the water, we cannot see it as solid.

This second type of compassion sees sentient beings as qualified by this kind of impermanence. They are understood to be impermanent. Just as in the first way of meditating compassion you didn't observe just sentient beings but sentient beings qualified by strong suffering, in this case you observe sentient beings qualified not just by strong suffering but also by impermanence.

It is said that, when you see the body of a person, its impermanence appears to your mind but your mind doesn't notice it; your mind doesn't apprehend it, doesn't realize it. Sitting in meditation and looking at a moon in shimmering water is a means of giving us a clear image of how we should begin to view others. The purpose of using this picture of evanescence is to expose our usual overlay of solidity in order to reveal what is actually there. In time you will be able to see such phenomena as walls and bodies in this way, composed of many particles moving. This shimmering, this evanescence, can become vivid to your own consciousness.

Through this image you can get a sense of what impermanence means so that you can then apply it to sentient beings. If you begin to see persons this way—as shimmering, evanescent—you realize that you view yourself and others as solid and that you construct relationships with people and things based on a solid body, a solid mind, a solid self, and thereby lead yourself into trouble, insisting on things that cannot be had. You realize that your view does not accord with reality.

You generate a wish to get out of such a wrong view, and when you apply this perspective to others, you generate compassion—the wish that they be freed from suffering. They too are misconceiving phenomena and, through this misconception, are being drawn into suffering.

When, through analytical meditation, a vivid sense of their pain due to misconceptions of permanence is manifest to you, within a sense of their similarity to and intimacy with you, take your best friend to mind. **Contemplate: "How nice it would be if this person were free from suffering and the causes of suffering!"** When a strong sense of compassion arises, stay with this deeply felt wish in stabilizing meditation. Then, pass on to your next best friend, and repeat the process in brief form or in more detail according to whether the feeling is generated easily or not. Then, continue by considering individual neutral persons, lesser enemies, and finally stronger enemies.

Then, using the same format, in meditation cultivate the second subjective level of compassion but this time based on realization of the impermanence of beings and their tendency to conceive just the opposite. Contemplate: "May they be free from suffering and the causes of suffering!" When you succeed with that, move to the third level of compassion. **Using the same format, contemplate: "I will free them from suffering and the causes of suffering."** The effects are powerful.

UNCONSCIOUS ASSUMPTIONS
OF PERMANENCE

We know that things disintegrate; we know, in some sense, that they are impermanent. If asked, "Are you permanent? Will you live forever?" none of us would say yes, and yet we live our lives as if we think we will live forever. There is a discrepancy between how we answer that question and the perspective within which we lead our lives, planning this and planning that. One of the reasons why things seem to be permanent is that there is often a similarity, a continuity of type. This kind of table was here yesterday. It didn't switch into being a blue table or a bigger one, and it didn't rot overnight, or change in any way that is discernible to us.

The continuity of type deceives us into thinking that the same thing is there, that we're meeting the exact same people. We think, "There's so-and-so that I saw the other day," and then, "John showed up yesterday, the one I knew last year." Because of the continuity of type, people and things seem to us to be the same, and this encourages the misperception that the table I use here today is the same one that I was using yesterday. It is said that even though its disintegration moment by moment is appearing to even our visual consciousness, we do not notice it because our predisposition for objects remaining the same is so great that it blocks out noticing this level of change.

We are often falsely reaffirmed in the sense of sameness. If you go back to your old high school, you find that the buildings are rather the same. You may feel a bit lost, but there are still people there, perhaps a few of the old teachers. The students look somewhat different, but they too are rather the same. You get a sense of solidity from the fact that there is continuity. But is there solidity in continuity? Continuity actually means that something is not solid, that it cannot remain for a second moment, that only something of a similar type can go on. I went back to my elementary school and found that the building had been torn down and nothing had been put in its place; there was just grass. We often make up substitutes for the truth. People say, "I will live on in my children," but how does one do this?

Have you ever watched birds closely? We generally think of them as being carefree, but when you observe them closely, you see that most of them are very nervous. Also, if you watch the sky, you can see that it changes tremendously; and the same with water, a stream or a river—it is constantly changing. When you stare at the center of a candle flame, which at first appears to be so steady, you see that it also is continuously changing. This continual change is true of everything.

One of my lamas repeatedly reminded us that everything is like this. We understand this on an intellectual level from studying physics, that all these little particles are constantly changing, but we don't see them as doing that; we're not aware of what is happening on the particle level in everyday life. We think that our emotional lives should be lived on a different basis. But Buddhism teaches you how to build an emotional life on subtle observation, to put into practice that kind of perception.

In the blink of an eye, everything is changing. Or, even more subtly, in each three-hundred-sixtieth of a blinking of an eye or of the snapping of the fingers, everything is disintegrating. For a Buddha, the realization of this is still more subtle, but at our level this measurement affords a glimpse of subtle change. It is said that all impermanent phenomena possess a nature of such subtle disintegration.

NATURAL IMPERMANENCE

We tend to think that things change because of something acting on them from the outside. For instance, we know that if we leave a piece of iron out in the elements, it will eventually rust and disintegrate, but we think that if it is encased in a vacuum, it will not change and will just remain as iron, as if it takes something coming from the outside to affect it, to cause it to change. But ultimately this is not so; the particles of iron keep changing even in the vacuum. Similarly, we often blame our illnesses of old age on various things coming at us from the outside, and sometimes those factors do act to cause changes in us, but even without any outside interference, disintegration is occurring moment by moment.

We persist in thinking that things are being acted on from the outside, that otherwise they would remain the same except for the interfering cause, whereas in reality, since things possess a nature of disintegration, nothing extraneous is required in order for them to disintegrate outside of the fact that they were produced in the first place. They need merely to be produced in order to disintegrate. The causes that produce objects are also the causes of disintegration—the causes of production *are* the causes of disintegration. This is one of the great insights of almost all Buddhist schools. In the higher teachings it is called uncaused disintegration, a truly profound and provocative notion. Of course, in terms of gross disintegration, there can be factors acting from outside that greatly hasten the process, like water on iron, or dynamiting a building. But remember that because of its very nature, the iron is, moment by moment, disintegrating; it just naturally disintegrates over time.

It is said to be difficult to understand this, to feel it, to realize it, to experience it, partly because we have to give up our preconceived notions about permanence and impermanence in order to see it. It can be frightening, so we have to develop patience, forbearance, and perseverance with respect to comprehending impermanence. Patience in this context means being able to stand it, having facility with it.

Returning to Chandrakirti's image: It's night, there's a full moon, clear sky, but a slight breeze is causing the water of the lake to ripple, so the reflection of the moon is very clear, but rippling, flickering. That is the image for impermanence— moon particles shimmering, bristling with impermanence. He uses this vision not merely as a metaphor, but as a method we can use to experience the impermanence of other things, and especially the way we view our own bodies.

Imagine the reflection of the moon in water, flickering, shimmering, so you can see it as particles, and you can see that the particles are flashing on and off, causing you to take

notice of their impermanence. Then shift your attention to your own body and see it the same way. You usually see your body as solid and constant and make many plans and have many wishes, and so forth, for a body and a person that don't flicker this way. Thus, when you start seeing your body as constantly changing, you have to give up the image of a constant body and a constant self with all the wishes and plans that go with it. You have to make new plans.

If you make plans around such a flickering person, you will be ready for the changes that naturally occur. Imagine such an evanescent person going about daily activities. Such a perspective is actually more effective because is it more realistic, more open to the changes that will occur and for which you will be unprepared if you are stuck in a false sense of constancy.

With this type of image of the fragility of your body, even the possibility of dying at any moment will be clear. By seeing that others are in the same precarious situation but often are unaware of it, your sense of compassion for them will increase. You will value the time you have as a precious treasure and will hope that others may value their own moments of life as much.

PLAYING WITH A NEW PERSPECTIVE

The question arises: Is this new way of viewing sentient beings right or wrong? You have played with it up to this point, but is it right or wrong? Is it helpful to view yourself and others this way, or is it harmful or perhaps just foolish? In order to find out, it may be helpful to continue playing with it. When I was defending my Ph.D. dissertation, one of the questioners seemed touched by what was being said, but his reaction was violent. We were talking about proving whether things inherently exist or not and setting up a certain number of possibilities: You have mind and body, and you have the I. The I seems to be substantial, and the mind and body seem to be substantial. We usually agree on their appearance of seeming substantiality. If the appearance is correct, if there are such concrete things, then what are the possible relationships between the I, on the one hand, and the mind and body on the other?

When I said that, the man exploded: "What are you doing? You're playing with my mind." And, indeed, if Buddhists were going to play with your mind, trick you, this is where they would.

I said, "Do you play Ping-Pong? Do you ever go to the movies? Do you ever entertain anything? How about entertaining this for a while? Just play with it; play with it from a Buddhist's point of view." He said, "What? It'll contaminate my mind."

I said, "Well, you go to the movies, and you pretend that the people on the screen are doing various things. Is that harmful?" He didn't even want to hear anything about it; he was not open at all. Still, to me it seemed that he was moved; there was something about this concept that struck him.

It helps to look at things from another person's point of view. Take, for example, a time when it's quite warm and a slight breeze is blowing. Some people would experience that breeze as very cool. They'd say, "There's a terrible draft on my neck." Sometimes, when two people are sleeping together, one wants two blankets and the other doesn't want anything but a sheet. "What's wrong with you? There must be something wrong with your mind!"

"What do you mean?"

"Nobody in the universe could experience this as cold. It's *hot*, period."

Physical constitution, the balance or imbalance of the elements in the body, makes people experience heat and cold differently.

In this case, looking at things from the other person's point of view could help. Though you won't reverse your opinion of whether it's cold for you, you may save the other person the torture of being accused of insanity because she or he feels cold now and then. In the cases of impermanence and compassion, too, it may be that we are holding the wrong idea and that, through entertaining someone else's idea, we can begin to understand the nature of that person's conviction. And *then* we can begin to examine it.

The most obvious problem is this: The Buddhists say, "All right, let's try this out, and start seeing sentient beings as evanescent, shimmering, impermanent." But how could we relate to beings? It's impossible; they are disappearing as soon as they appear. They are changing too much. Maybe there is value in seeing them as solid—even though they are not solid—in order to relate to them more easily.

I think this is basically why we see persons and other phenomena as solid. It seems—it *seems*—that it is easier to relate to them if they appear solid, but in fact it will become easier to relate to them when you see them as evanescent, because their evanescence is a display of their impermanence, and by seeing this, you won't be surprised by their changes; you won't lock people into certain patterns of behavior and then, because you see them as solid, influence them to stay in those patterns. You will see potential for change, and others may experience your own presence as pleasantly open, because you aren't superimposing fixed patterns contrary to reality on them.

Reflection on impermanence reveals the gap between how we conceive ourselves and how we actually are. We see that this disparity itself draws us into repeated pain by forcing us to try to satisfy a sense of selfhood and possessions that actually does not exist. Through this route, the more we reflect on impermanence, the deeper and more forceful our compassion becomes.

COMPASSION SEEING
EMPTY BEINGS

Meditation: The Reflection of the Moon in a Calm Lake

T HE THIRD TYPE of compassion is called compassion seeing empty beings—sentient beings empty of existing in
and of themselves, independently. Chandrakirti says:

Homage to that compassion for transmigrating beings
Seen as empty of inherent existence,
Like a moon in calm water.

**In meditation, imagine a calm lake on a cloudless night. A
full moon is reflected in the water, but you don't know that
a lake is there. You actually are looking at the reflection of a
moon in water, but you think you are seeing the moon.**

Have you ever come by a lake at night when there isn't any
wind? You see a moon reflected on the smooth surface of the
water and think it is the moon? It happened to me once when
I didn't know a lake was there, and upon seeing what actually

was the near side of the lake, I thought I was looking at the horizon. Haven't you unexpectedly passed by a mirror in a store and, seeing yourself, thought it was somebody else? Or been unable to place the walls of a mirrored restaurant for a while? In an airport shop in Australia, I looked over at a fellow and thought, "Who's that seedy fellow over there?" It was my reflection.

You don't see water; you see the moon, surrounded by sky—that's how it seems. Like pictures that look the same in opposite positions. You turn the picture one way and see mountains with a lake reflecting them, and you turn it the other way and see mountains with a lake reflecting them, and you can't decide which are the actual mountains and which the reflection. In Chandrakirti's example, if you take a good look at the moon without superimposing the thought, "This is just a reflection in water," you see something that appears to have every characteristic of a moon. Similarly, if you look in a mirror and cancel out the thought, "This is a mirror," then, when you look closely and slowly, there is something in front of you that has all the appearance of being a face. Yet the reflection of a moon in water is not a moon; the reflection of a face in a mirror is not a face.

Chandrakirti is advising that we gain experience with this type of example. He is not being facile, presenting a brilliant example and letting us pass on to the next subject. Rather, he is suggesting that we engage in reflection, analysis, and meditation, asking us to imagine a moon in water to see that the reflection appears to be the object whereas it is not—so that we can develop an intimately experienced model of a conflict between appearance and reality. First we need to explore the false appearance as if we did not know it was false. Stare at a mirror long enough and exactly that happens.

A reflection of the moon in water appears to be a moon but is not. Sentient beings appear to exist inherently but do not. When you get used to looking at the moon in water, seeing from every side that it is not a moon although it appears to be, then, when you look at a sentient being, you can use this as an introduction to the fact that, although you experience a person that seems to exist from the person's own side, this is not the case.

An illusion created by a magician is another common example of a false appearance. In India, there are magicians who work with a rope and a boy. One was brought to the United States, and a film made of this act in a laboratory. The rope magically uncoiled and went up into space, and the boy climbed to the top of the rope. It wasn't hanging from anything. All the doctors in the room saw the boy climb the rope, but the camera saw the boy standing next to a man with a coiled rope. The magician had the power to affect the spectators' eye consciousness so that they saw the boy climb the rope even though he didn't.

Buddhists describe the magician as using the power of mantra to cast a spell on the eyes of all present. Everyone sees the boy climb the rope. The magician also sees the boy climb the rope, but he doesn't believe the appearance at all. He knows that the boy is standing next to him and that the rope is coiled on the floor. He sees the illusion vividly, just as vividly as the others; the others believe it, but he does not.

In another example, a magician creates a feast. As a member of the audience, you would think, "There's some super chocolate cake. How can I get it? Should I rush up faster than the others?" Or the magician creates an attractive male or female, and you think, "That's just the kind of person I've always wanted. How can we meet?" You enter into many thoughts— desire and maybe hatred: "Someone else is looking too." The magician sees the beautiful girl or fellow but does not enter into any of these thoughts because of knowing the nature of the appearance. The audience, however, enters into these thoughts. Then some persons come along who were not there when the magician was casting the mantra into everyone's eyes; they do not see the illusion; they enter into no thoughts about such an ideal mate. Unlike the magician, they don't even see the false appearance—they see just the fact. Thus, the audience is compared to ordinary persons overwhelmed by appearances; the magician is compared to someone who has overcome belief in the false appearances, who knows what appears is empty of the status it seems to have, but who still is subject to the appearances; and those who came late and are not affected by the mantra of illusion are compared to Buddhas who have overcome all ignorance. Similarly, meditation on such examples aids in realizing that persons, bodies, and other phenomena appear to have a concrete status that they actually do not have, that they are empty of such solidity. This is what is meant by "empty beings."

IS EVERYTHING ACTUALLY SO CONCRETE?

Like the illusory appearances, sentient beings appear to exist inherently, by way of their own character, of their own nature, as if covering a certain spot. That is undeniable. Everybody seems to cover a certain spot. I cover a certain spot, although, from my own point of view, the spot I cover is different from the one you think I cover. You may look at my body, whereas I'm thinking mainly of the mind or feeling or breath, and that is why, if someone came in and asked, "Who is going to do such and such?" and I answered, "*I'm* going to do it." I might feel I was pointing to my chest; if you pointed at me, you would probably point to the whole body.

The face in the mirror appears to be a face, but it is not a face from any point of view. Similarly, an inherently existent person, existing right here with mind and body, in and of itself, doesn't exist, but such an inherently existent person appears to exist. Emptiness doesn't mean there are no people and that therefore you don't need to be compassionate. That's not what it means. *No!* That's silly. Emptiness means people don't exist in the concrete way we imagine them to. Myself. Yourself. We don't exist so solidly. For example, a table appears to cover the area of its bases of designation—the collection of the top, legs, and so forth—but no such table exists there. Still, this does not mean that there is no table at all. We have to determine what the example is exemplifying—the illusory appearance of inherent existence. This is not a doctrine of nonexistence in general but a doctrine of the nonexistence of a certain type of false, overconcretized existence; it does not deny all existence. Realization of impermanence helps toward realizing that persons and other phenomena are empty of such concreteness, but the realization of emptiness is more subtle.

The Dalai Lama advises that you do this type of meditation on a person or other phenomenon that you value highly, since the experience of emptiness will not be misinterpreted as a devaluing of the subject—the value will remain high but be seen a different way. During a period when he was teaching me in his office in India, my experience was particularly intense. One late afternoon, for instance, as I looked at him across his desk with a set of windows stretching behind him, the sun was fairly low on the horizon in Kangra Valley. The topic was the stages of death—a profound presentation of deeper stages of the mind on which not just death but all conscious experience is built. The teacher was this person who, in Tibetan, has incredible powers of speech—very fast and very clear at the same time—and brings a vast array of teaching to bear on a single topic. The scene was the brilliant glow of the sun across a vivid orange sky—like the second stage of the four subtle minds experienced when dying, going to sleep, fainting, and so forth. I felt as "at home" as I ever could in my life. Then, as I stepped out of his office, I was stunned, looking up at the snow-covered peak above Dharamsala. I began walking to my room farther down the mountain, passing an area where there is a mountain on the other side, too. The space between the two mountains was filled with a circular rainbow—a complete circle. I was amazed! Several days later as I was leaving after my last class with the Dalai Lama, preparing to return to the States, he said as I stepped near the door, "It is like a dream." I said, "What?" "It's like a dream." The realism, at once stark and rich, was stunning. He had caused me to reflect on the emptiness of this most effective and valuable period of my life. Emptiness does not cancel phenomena; rather, it is compatible with effectiveness, with value.

First, gain the experience of slowly looking over the image of the reflection of the moon—this is a profound essential—going over every part of it, realizing that every part of it is not a moon, that the whole thing together is not a moon, that there is nothing there at all which is a moon. Then, remaining in that experience of a vivid appearance of a moon but the utter lack of a moon, view sentient beings or other phenomena and, becoming like a magician, understand that the object, however vividly it appears, does not exist inherently, even though it appears to exist in its own right. Understand that phenomena arise dependent on their causes and conditions and arise dependent on their parts such that they could not possibly exist in and of themselves as they seem to do. Eventually the false part of the appearance itself fades, leaving only the actual object for your mind's eye.

How does such a perspective on the nature of appearances serve to generate compassion? If you see that sentient beings perceive themselves one way and yet exist another way and thereby are drawn into suffering in order to satisfy this kind of self when there is no such self—no *such* self, not that there is no self—if you see that at least certain desires and certain hatreds are predicated on this kind of self and that people are leading themselves into trouble because of it, you naturally generate compassion for them if you have a sense of closeness with them, a sense of empathy. Through realizing, "I want happiness and don't want suffering, and each of these people wants happiness and doesn't want suffering; how horrible it is that what they want and what they are engaged in are at cross-purposes!"—that they want happiness and don't want suffering but are engaging in causes of suffering which take them farther away from happiness—wouldn't you find it moving?

The example of the reflection of the moon in calm water is a means to experience, in a coarse way, the lack of correspondence between what appears so clearly but actually does not exist that way. When you switch from contemplating and feeling the impact of the metaphor to contemplating how phenomena appear in such a concrete way as if they existed in their own right, the force of the metaphor carries over, and you are propelled into glimpsing the discrepancy between appearance and reality. With such a perception as a basis, your sense of concern for beings so deeply deluded strengthens since you see a fundamental process by which we bring pain on ourselves.

COMPASSION AND WISDOM COMBINED

T HE WORLD is full of suffering—we see many pictures of people starving; often when we feel we can't do anything about it, we don't want to think about it. Why? Often it is because we would be too deeply moved and sense that we would be paralyzed by our own feelings of commiseration. During lectures when the Dalai Lama talks about compassion, he begins with "All sentient beings," and pauses. You can feel that he is extending his thought to many different types of beings. His voice cracks a little. Sometimes there are tears. It is as though he is saying, "Don't be afraid; don't hold back from such deep feelings."

There was a bodhisattva whose name was Always Crying because he was so concerned about the plight of sentient beings. The story is told to show how much reflecting on the suffering of other beings can impact on you. Still, the point is to develop a better mind, and if, in the process of doing so, you become full of worry, how can you help other sentient beings?

There is a difference between intelligent concern and worry. We often falsely associate concern with unbridled worry; we fancy that compassion necessarily turns us into blithering idiots. We refuse to open ourselves to great compassion due to associating it with something with which it need not be associated. However, when we realize *why* people suffer, we can see that at least some of their pain can be eliminated, and if it can be, then it is most touching that they suffer unnecessarily. With this understanding as background, we can allow ourselves to be moved by others' pain.

In this way, realization of the emptiness of a misconceived sense of inherent existence is a cause for the generation of compassion. If you begin to understand the causes of wandering in cyclic existence, the causes of anguish, you get a sense that these can be eliminated, for it is through an error of mind that these sufferings take place. It is difficult to generate the conviction that *all* suffering is caused by such error, but you can generate the conviction that at least some of it is.

When you see how deep the misconception of inherent existence is, when you see how pervasive its effects are, you can see how, from this one small error, huge problems are produced. It is really poignant. But because there is a way out, we can allow ourselves to open up to deep feelings of commiseration.

You can see the compatibility of emptiness and compassion. It is most certainly not the case that Buddhists become compassionate and then, upon understanding "emptiness," neglect everything. Realization of emptiness is a tool for the enhancement of compassion, and further, it is a tool for the development of a mind that will be able to bring about the welfare of beings, because one will no longer be deceived by their nature. The wisdom that comes with realizing emptiness enhances compassion. You see your own suffering (or at least much of it) as caused by the false apprehension that persons and other phenomena exist in their own right, and you see the similarly caused suffering of all other beings, and since they are close to you, you wish—from the bottom of your heart—to relieve them of their pain. In this way, love and compassion become founded in perception of reality, unlike ordinary limited love which often arises from exaggerating the pleasantness of the other person and thus easily disappears or flips to unconcern or even anger with surprising alacrity.

You need a long-term sense that, even if it takes eons—lifetime after lifetime—you'll be willing to do anything to help even one particular person. Still, being moved does not necessarily entail external action right now. Within constant compassion, you can make more intelligent decisions about whether it's better to keep interacting with the person or whether it's better to quietly get out the door, or to ask the other person to get out the door. "For the time being, right now, it seems that whatever I do makes the situation worse." This doesn't mean you're eliminating that person from the count of those beings who are close to you.

One of the biggest problems is to remove someone from the count of sentient beings, to remove someone from that group of people who are like yourself. Kensur Lekden said, "You are like a child of all sentient beings. All sentient beings have been extremely kind to you, have taken care of you. If my parents of this lifetime had not taken care of me, I would be unable to talk, unable to study, unable to make progress. In past lifetimes, all sentient beings have taken care of me. Therefore, I am like a child of all sentient beings. All sentient beings are like your parents when they are old, and who will take care of them if their own children do not?" You feel this type of closeness with all sentient beings, as their child. We have responsibility for each other; we cannot act out of mere self-centeredness.

With wisdom and compassion working together, feelings of empathy and commiseration are built on the strength of valid realization of the nature of persons and things, and analytical intelligence is warm to the feelings of both oneself and others. For the time being, these two sides have to balance each other, but in the end they are so intertwined that they are indistinguishable. Other-concern makes happy sense.

SELECTED READINGS

The Dalai Lama
H.H. the Dalai Lama. *Kindness, Clarity, and Insight.* Translated and edited by Jeffrey Hopkins; coedited by Elizabeth Napper. Revised ed. Ithaca, N.Y.: Snow Lion Publications, 2006.
———. *The Meaning of Life.* Translated and edited by Jeffrey Hopkins. Boston: Wisdom Publications, 2000.

Kensur Lekden
Lekden, Kensur. *Meditations of a Tibetan Tantric Abbot.* Translated and edited by Jeffrey Hopkins. Ithaca, N.Y.: Snow Lion Publications, 2001.

Nagarjuna
Hopkins, Jeffrey. *Nagarjuna's Precious Garland: Buddhist Advice for Living and Liberation.* Ithaca, N.Y.: Snow Lion Publications, 2007.

Shantideva
Shantideva. *A Guide to the Bodhisattva Way of Life.* Translated by Vesna A. Wallace and B. Alan Wallace. Ithaca, N.Y.: Snow Lion Publications, 1997.